THE BRITISH MAZE GUIDE

Adrian Fisher & Jeff Saward

The Saxon Maze
The Herb Farm, Sonning Common

Acknowledgements

Pictures
Blenheim Palace - 19.
Adrian Fisher - front cover, 1, 6, 17, 20-1, 24-5, 28-30, 32, 36, 39, 44-5, 47, 49-53, 55-7, 60-1, 64-6, 71, 74, back cover.
W H Matthews - 22, 70.
Jeff Saward - 5, 8-9, 15, 18, 38, 41, 58-9, 63.
Heyward Sumner - 23.

First Edition
Copyright 1991, Adrian Fisher and Jeff Saward
ISBN 0 9517468 0 4

Published by Minotaur Designs, 42 Brampton Road, St Alban's, Hertfordshire, AL1 4PT, England (0727 44800; internationally 44 727 44800).
Typeset by Minotaur Designs. Printed by Color Craft, Hong Kong.

For a uniquely designed maze, of any materials, anywhere in the world, please contact Minotaur Designs at the above address.

Full-size indoor and outdoor Minotaur Colour Mazes, Maze Books, Games, Hardwood Puzzles and other maze merchandise are also available from Minotaur Designs at the above address.

Tapestry Kits of Minotaur mazes are available from: Royal School of Needlework, Mail Order Dept, Little Barrington, Burford, Oxfordshire, OX8 4TE (tel.0451 4433); also Luxury Needlepoint Ltd, 324 Kings St, Hammersmith, London, W6 0RR (tel. 081 741 1314).

Telephone numbers are given in the guide, in case visitors wish to check opening times before setting out.

All possible care has been taken to trace and acknowledge illustrations, and to check details of each maze. If errors have accidentally occurred, or telephone numbers have changed, the publishers will be happy to correct them in future editions, provided they receive notification.

The British Maze Guide

Adrian Fisher & Jeff Saward

Contents

FRONT COVER *The low box maze, Hatfield House*
FRONTISPIECE *The Saxon Maze, The Herb Farm, Sonning Common*
BACK COVER *The Magical Mirror Maze, Wookey Hole Caves, Somerset*

The Diversity of British M

This guide sets out to celebrate the variety and
mazes and labyrinths scattered throughout the Bri
spirit, examples within the Republic of Ireland are

Britain has more mazes open to the public than an
Europe, having increased from forty in 1980 to
today. Sweden has greater numbers, with over th
lined path labyrinths scattered along the Baltic c
them lie on off-shore islands only accessible by bo
150 wooden mazes, all of them built since 1984,
had an unprecedented maze craze which has since

Britain's gentle climate, warmed by the Atlanti
always encouraged and rewarded her gardeners.
and flourish, and turf mazes are easy to maintain
at Hampton Court Palace is the most famous thr
speaking world, and indeed the 300th annivers
provided the inspiration for Britain's "Year of th

Many of Britain's recent mazes respond to our c
with enigmatic delights in town parks and
wherever the spirit of childhood can find a cha
distinguishes Britain is the sheer diversity and
mazes, including examples made with brick,
water, wood, mosaic, stained glass and mirrors,

We hope this guide will stimulate a renewed f
from greater appreciation of ancient turf labyrint
greens and enjoyment of puzzle hedge mazes,
modern symbolic mazes as a vibrant garden an

We urge you to savour these unusual creation
shall have succeeded if an ecclesiastical labyrin
appreciate its architectural setting, a turf m
unspoilt village green, or an enigmatic roc
completely off the beaten track.

The British Maze Guide

Adrian Fisher & Jeff Saward

Contents

FRONT COVER *The low box maze, Hatfield House*
FRONTISPIECE *The Saxon Maze, The Herb Farm, Sonning Common*
BACK COVER *The Magical Mirror Maze, Wookey Hole Caves, Somerset*

The Diversity of British Mazes

This guide sets out to celebrate the variety and originality of the mazes and labyrinths scattered throughout the British Isles. In this spirit, examples within the Republic of Ireland are also included.

Britain has more mazes open to the public than any other country in Europe, having increased from forty in 1980 to over one hundred today. Sweden has greater numbers, with over three hundred stone-lined path labyrinths scattered along the Baltic coast, but many of them lie on off-shore islands only accessible by boat. Japan has about 150 wooden mazes, all of them built since 1984, when that country had an unprecedented maze craze which has since passed its peak.

Britain's gentle climate, warmed by the Atlantic gulf stream, has always encouraged and rewarded her gardeners. Hedge mazes grow and flourish, and turf mazes are easy to maintain. The hedge maze at Hampton Court Palace is the most famous throughout the English speaking world, and indeed the 300th anniversary of its planting provided the inspiration for Britain's "Year of the Maze" in 1991.

Many of Britain's recent mazes respond to our contemporary society with enigmatic delights in town parks and paved city centres, wherever the spirit of childhood can find a chance to play. What distinguishes Britain is the sheer diversity and imagination of her mazes, including examples made with brick, stone, gravel, turf, water, wood, mosaic, stained glass and mirrors, as well as hedges.

We hope this guide will stimulate a renewed fascination in mazes, from greater appreciation of ancient turf labyrinths on English village greens and enjoyment of puzzle hedge mazes, to the recognition of modern symbolic mazes as a vibrant garden and landscape art-form.

We urge you to savour these unusual creations one at a time; we shall have succeeded if an ecclesiastical labyrinth encourages you to appreciate its architectural setting, a turf maze takes you to an unspoilt village green, or an enigmatic rock carving leads you completely off the beaten track.

Origins of the Labyrinth

The Labyrinth symbol and the legends surrounding it are among the most ancient known. It is found scattered around the world amongst different cultures and during different periods in history; throughout, the symbol itself remains unchanged and the traditions connected with it are remarkably constant.

Whilst mazes can have dead ends, false pathways and choices to confuse, true labyrinths consist of a single meandering pathway which leads inexorably from the entrance to the centre, and on occasions back out again. This 'unicursal' (one-pathway) form was the only form used for thousands of years; later 'multicursal' mazes familiar to everyone as hedge or puzzle mazes only appeared after the Middle Ages. Considering that 'unicursal' labyrinths provide no puzzle, and that these labyrinths do not conceal the goal from view, but are usually just marked upon the ground by shallow trenches or stones, the question of their purpose springs instantly to mind.

Turf and stone labyrinths are found throughout north-western Europe, and while some are of comparatively recent construction, some of these stone labyrinths found in Scandinavia could be as much as 3,000 years old. Their conformity in design is remarkable, for although local variations and expansions of the design do occur, most are of the same ancient type, or a direct derivation from it. This design is found in ancient contexts throughout the world, in a number of different mediums and serving a number of different roles and usages, as far apart as India, Iceland, Sumatra and Arizona.

The Classical labyrinth

The labyrinth design became widespread in north-western Europe, becoming a living monument in the landscape, as opposed to a symbol within a mythology, as the sites of at least 125 turf and 500 stone labyrinths attest. Few survive, particularly those built in turf.

What is the fascination hidden in this design that has transported it around the world and through thousands of years? The purpose and usage is relatively clear, for in many cultures including Europe, the labyrinth has been used as a ceremonial pathway and as a dancing ground. The twisting, tortuous paths guard the central goal from direct penetration, for here the souls of the dead ancestors were thought to reside, barred from escaping to cause trouble in the local community. In Sweden, Baltic fishing crews would run the labyrinths before setting sail, to trap the evil spirits and unfavourable winds that might otherwise follow them out to sea. Throughout Europe young women would stand at the centre of the labyrinth as suitors chased through the windings to seek out their potential bride. Running through the expanding and contracting circuits mimicked the path of the sun across the sky, recognising the repeated rebirth of the sun each morning and each year. As many stories are told as mythologies exist, but in all, the labyrinth seems to symbolise the path to be followed, in daily and seasonal cycles, in life, in death and in rebirth.

The origin of the labyrinth, both as a symbol and as a concept, has often been connected with the ruined Minoan temple/palace complex at Knossos. Ariadne's thread, the clew, was the means by which Theseus entered the legendary Cretan Labyrinth, despatched the unfortunate Minotaur and retraced his steps unscathed, thus symbolically breaking the domination of King Minos of Knossos over the city of Athens. Historically, the demise of Crete occurred in the 15th century BC. Whatever the truth of this myth, Cretan coins of the first century BC carried the seven-ring Classical labyrinth design.

Many clues remain to help unravel and understand the lure of the labyrinth design, not least the method of its construction.

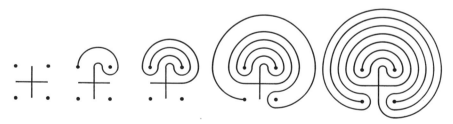

Method of construction of the Classical labyrinth

With practice, a perfect labyrinth can be drawn every time. Indeed the simplicity of this method may account for the universal distribution of the labyrinth design. Many varieties of labyrinth design actually encountered in antiquity can be produced by adaptation of the basic method of construction, suggesting that this was how the labyrinth symbol was learnt and passed on throughout its history.

This seven-ring labyrinth design is known as the "Classical" type, due to its occurrence as the most ancient and widespread labyrinth form. The earliest attested date of the labyrinth symbol is c. 1200 BC for an inscribed clay tablet found at Pylos, Greece, and c. 1300 BC for several labyrinth decorated pottery fragments from Tell Rifa'at, Syria. A number of labyrinths carved on rockfaces throughout Europe could conceivably be older, but effective dating techniques do not exist.

Ultimately, the origin of the labyrinth remains a mystery. If it was first conceived of c. 1500 BC, in the wake of the Minoan palaces, then how can one account for labyrinths carved on rockfaces in Arizona, and labyrinths carved on the gold finger-rings and timbers of houses among remote jungle dwelling tribes in Sumatra? Could the design be so ancient that it spread around the globe during the earliest migrations of people to Indonesia and the Americas? Possibly the mathematical properties of the design are such that it has been independently discovered at different times by different peoples.

The labyrinth symbol was popular among the Romans, and Pliny records that they were familiar with turf labyrinths. They used the labyrinth extensively for mosaic pavements. Many are encircled by a representation of a city wall, an allusion to the city of Troy, long connected with the labyrinth. Throughout Europe ancient labyrinths are known as "City of Troy" or "Walls of Troy", although whether in reference to the ritual employed to breach the walls of the legendary city, or for some more ancient reason is unclear. The Welsh word "troi" - to turn - hints at a more complex origin to the connection between Troy and the labyrinth. Roman labyrinths were more complex than the earlier Classical type, and were designed more to please the eye than for walking or running as a ritual dance.

The History of Mazes in Britain

Ancient Labyrinths

The earliest labyrinths in the British Isles were probably of the seven-ring Classical design, created as stone-lined paths or cut in turf; however, both these methods of construction are easily damaged or destroyed, and impossible to date once disturbed.

Britain's oldest datable labyrinths are made of Roman mosaic. The labyrinth motif was used in mosiac pavements throughout the Roman Empire, and about fifty have been found dating between 100 BC and 400 AD. Of these, six are in Britain, including those now on display at the Caerleon Legionary Museum in Gwent (second/third century), and in Hull City Hall (early fourth century).

Roman mosaic labyrinth, Caerleon

Ireland's Hollywood Stone, c. 550 AD, is probably the earliest rock-carved labyrinth in the British Isles; the two rock carvings in the Rocky Valley near Tintagel, found in 1942 but impossible to date, may well be late 17th century. Also in the south west, the Scilly Isles possess Britain's best examples of stone-ring labyrinths; whilst this form can date back a thousand years or more in Scandinavia, the oldest British example, on St Agnes, may be as recent as 1729.

England contained many unicursal turf mazes, some possibly created during the Dark Ages by nordic invaders and settlers. Turf mazes are constructed simply by taking an area of turf, and cutting out gullies to form the barrier; the remaining upstanding turf becomes the path. Their names Troytown and Walls of Troy recall the seige of Troy and the penetration of its walls by deception, whilst Shepherd's Race and Robin Hood's Race imply vigorous running.

In thirteenth century France, Medieval Christian pavement mazes, with eleven rings of paths, were laid in the stone floors of gothic cathedrals; names such as Chemin de Jerusalem reflected recent journeys of the Crusades. In proceeding along its path, one could contemplate the thread of time, and the path of life through death to salvation.

Chartres Cathedral Pavement Maze

In England, the Medieval Christian labyrinth design never appeared inside ecclesiastical buildings. Many English turf mazes may have been cut at this time, or recut to the Medieval Christian design to banish their earlier pagan origins.

In Shakespeare's time turf mazes were still in active use, as can be discerned from "A Midsummer Night's Dream" (Act II, Scene I):

'The nine men's morris is fill'd up with mud,

And the quaint mazes in the wanton green

For lack of tread, are undistinguishable.'

This speech was complaining about the weather, and not implying that turf mazes were in decline, as some writers have suggested.

In 1660, the monarchy was restored, and turf mazes were revived, for example at Hilton in Cambridgeshire where an inscribed pillar was erected to record its restoration. Over one hundred possible British turf maze sites have been detected, of which forty are known with certainty, yet only eight of these ancient turf mazes survive.

Garden Mazes

During the Middle Ages, formal gardens began to be established throughout Europe, enclosed for protection against the foraging of wild animals, and to provide shelter for better cultivation.

Early mazes often had royal connections. Henry II is reputed to have kept his mistress, the Fair Rosamund, in an unusual labyrinth at Woodstock Park; however, in about 1176, Queen Eleanor tricked her way into this labyrinth of stout walls and doors and forced the girl to choose between a dagger or poison; she drank the poison, and it is said that the king never smiled again. The site is marked today by a well and fountain in the grounds of Blenheim Palace.

By 1494 "a knot in a garden, called a mase" had become a commonly understood expression in England. Many early garden mazes were unicursal, with low plant-filled barriers, and were decorative rather than puzzles. Like knot gardens, they formed attractive patterns that could be appreciated close up, or from a raised surrounding walk or upstairs window. Often planted with fragrant herbs, evergreen plants ensured year round visual interest. Dwarf Box is not known to have been used until 1603.

The royal maze at Nonsuch Palace in Surrey was described in an early record in 1599 as having hedges so tall that one could not see over them. Similarly, at Theobalds in Hertfordshire, Lord Burghley had a garden hedge maze constructed about 1560, but it was destroyed in 1643 by rampaging troops during the English Civil War, *"demolish'd by the rebels"* according to John Evelyn in his *Memoirs*. Despite having hedges, both these mazes were unicursal, and probably the scope for concealing a puzzle was not appreciated.

William III built the famous hedge maze at Hampton Court Palace about 1690, having created one in 1682 at Het Loo Palace in Holland. Since then, the Hampton Court maze has inspired hedge mazes throughout the English speaking world, including those at Tatton Park (1890), Albert Park in Middlesborough (1894), Mentmore Towers (1899), Knebworth House and Castle Bromwich Hall.

In the late seventeenth century, "block" hedge mazes appeared; rather than having hedges of uniform width, the paths ran through thick blocks of shrubs. The block maze formerly at Trinity College Oxford was removed in 1813, and there were others at Belvoir Castle, Boughton, Exton Park, Badminton and Castle Howard.

Between 1818 and 1830, the 4th Lord Stanhope planted a maze at Chevening to a design by the 2nd Earl (1714-1786) who was an eminent mathematician. The design was highly innovative, taking maze puzzlement to the most complex two-dimensional form possible; in Victorian times, this maze design was copied at Anerley Park, North Woolwich and at Beauport House near Hastings. By contrast, in 1833 Alfred Fox planted a delightfully informal laurel maze with sinuous hedges on the side of a valley at Glendurgan in Cornwall.

The 'Italianate' style of gardening became popular during the 1840s; such schemes often involved a hedge maze, such as at Shrublands Hall and Bridge End Gardens in Saffron Walden (1839). The maze at Somerleyton Hall (1846) has a central oriental pavilion; a replica of the Somerleyton Maze was planted at Worden Park, Lancashire (1886). A Chinese influence prevailed at Woburn Abbey, whose maze with its delightful painted pavilion is in the private gardens. Also in the private gardens, the strictly rectangular yew maze at Hatfield House (1840) is thought to replace an earlier maze.

Victorian hedge mazes were also built in public parks such as Saltwell Park, Gateshead, the Royal Horticultural Society's Gardens in South Kensington (1851), and at the Crystal Palace (1865), and in public pleasure gardens such as Ranelagh Gardens, Vauxhall Gardens and Beulah Spa, all in London, and the Rosherville Gardens, Gravesend. Hedge mazes were created in private gardens, and the British enthusiasm for mazes spread to Australia and the United States. In England, Christian pavement mazes appeared in Ely Cathedral (1870), and the churches of Itchen Stoke (1866), Bourn (1875) and Alkborough (1887).

In the twentieth century, the social and economic upheaval of two world wars imposed harsh neglect on existing gardens. For half a century it was difficult to maintain gardens let alone develop them, and many existing mazes were abandoned whilst few new ones were created. In 1922, W. H. Matthews was begging "Let us at any rate see to it that no more of these rare and interesting heirlooms are lost to us through ignorance or neglect". The book he wrote eventually proved to be a key factor in reviving interest in the subject.

The Modern Revival

Since the 1970's, there has been a renewed interest in mazes worldwide. In Britain, the number of mazes open to the public has increased from forty in 1980 to over one hundred mazes today. The elements of fun, puzzlement and discovery continue to fascinate. Mazes invite exploration and wonder, and like all the best games, are astonishingly simple in concept. They also have advantages over other attractions; visitors can make their own choices and proceed at their own pace, and they don't have to queue up to join in the fun.

Contemporary mazes have been created in many new settings, from pedestrian precincts to inner city parks, as well as stately homes, zoos and theme parks. They are found outdoors made of hedges, turf, brick, stone, wood and water; indoors, mazes of mosiac, marble, stained-glass and even mirrors and fountains have been created.

Modern British mazes contain unprecedented innovations, many pioneered most recently by Adrian Fisher and Lesley Beck of Minotaur Designs. Randoll Coate conceived the art of Multi-Layered Imagery, whereby a single maze design delineates various superimposed tableaux. In some fifteen mazes, Randoll and Adrian together developed the concept of Total Symbolism, so that the fun of solving the puzzle is heightened by the discovery of hidden meanings, expressed through shapes and juxtapositions, numbers, proportions, enigmatic inscriptions and symbolic artefacts. Symbolic Mazes have proved remarkably versatile at conveying ideas, from the contemplative Archbishop's Maze at Greys Court abounding in Christian symbolism, to the surreal Beatles' Maze (now destroyed) with its 18 ton Yellow Submarine, which captured the imagination of the people of Liverpool at the 1984 International Garden Festival.

The outline of a symbolic maze is powerful and compelling, especially when portraying a spectacular shape - such as that of a dragon, a steam engine, or a giant footprint. The lines of hedges within the maze also produce images on a huge scale, which can be seen dramatically from an aircraft. This is strikingly achieved by the Marlborough Maze at Blenheim Palace, by the Alice-in-Wonderland Maze at Merritown House and the Leeds Castle Maze in Kent.

The nature of puzzlement has also developed. Turf mazes have been transformed by introducing crossovers, junctions and one-way rules, such as at Parham Park, which make them into puzzle mazes. Several modern hedge mazes have a quick exit route, sometimes involving a bridge, as at Scone Palace and Merritown House, but none more exotic than the underground grotto and secret tunnel at Leeds Castle. Adrian Fisher's Colour Mazes have proved versatile at providing a challenging puzzle in a small space, whether laid in brick as at Leicester University, in paving tiles within a shopping mall, or in coloured plastic tiles at such varied locations as Flambards Theme Park, Drusillas Zoo Park and Blenheim Palace.

New forms of maze construction have also been pioneered. Modern turf mazes tend to use grass as the barrier, providing a hard path of brick or stone to bear the sheer weight of numbers. On paved surfaces, the sensational effect of "brick pavement mosaic" involves the cutting and laying of paving bricks in the same way as mosaic tesserae, but on a gigantic scale; examples include the Tudor Rose Maze at Kentwell Hall and the heraldic Lion and Unicorn mazes in Worksop. The pavement maze at Leicester University was laid without mortar on a bed of sand, with paving bricks simply butted tightly together and vibrated into place. Hedge mazes have been created on a larger scale than ever before, with the world's two largest hedge mazes at Longleat and Blenheim Palace. Britain now has a sensational mirror maze at Wookey Hole Caves, where optical illusions and fountains dancing to music create a memorable effect. Randoll Coate's Gaze-Maze concept was first demonstrated in the Bath Maze within a central mosaic, where, in each of seven sections, a thread of coloured mosaic is traced by eye around various images.

The diversity of Britain's mazes is unparalleled anywhere in the world, and the maze as a contemporary form of landscape and garden art is currently enjoying an explosive burst of evolution.

Yet perhaps the simplest way to experience its compelling mystery is to go and walk, or preferably run, through one of the ancient labyrinths that still exist in the British Isles. You will be repeating the unicursal journey that has survived virtually unchanged for thousands of years.

Guide to British Mazes

Mazes are listed alphabetically by location. The initial summary paragraph is taken from the Minotaur World Maze Database, which sets out to provide an up-to-date record of mazes and labyrinths worldwide, both past and present.

Aberdeen - *Hazlehead Maze, Hazlehead Park, Aberdeen, Scotland (tel. City Arts Department 0224 267267); privet hedges, rectangular, 190 x 160 ft; built by Sir Henry Alexander, 1935.*

Alkborough Cemetery - *Alkborough, South Humberside, England (O.S. Ref. SE 880214); gravestone in west corner of village cemetery, which is 600 yards SSW of the church; Medieval Christian labyrinth on metal plaque, on gravestone of Mr J Goulton-Constable, a keen maintainer of the Alkborough turf maze; erected 1922.*

Alkborough Church - *Alkborough, South Humberside (O.S. Ref. SE 882219); eleven-ring Medieval Christian design, stone pavement maze, circular, 6 x 6 ft, built 1887; also nineteenth century stained-glass east window, portraying labyrinth four inches wide.*

Upon the floor of the porch of the parish church, less than 300 yards from the turf maze, is engraved a 6 foot wide copy of the turf maze, the 'walls' of the design filled with dark cement. This was created in 1887 during a restoration of the church by Mr. J. Goulton-Constable, then lord of the manor, to ensure that the design of the turf maze would be preserved should it ever become overgrown. Also to be found inside the church is a stained glass window above the altar with a small replica of the design inset into one of the uppermost panes and a number of embroidered kneeling cushions, some bearing the labyrinth design. The church is open at all reasonable times.

Alkborough Turf Maze - *"Julian's Bower", Alkborough, South Humberside, England (O.S. Ref. SE 880218); eleven-ring Medieval Christian design; turf paths, circular, 44 x 44 ft; date unknown; open at all times.*

"Julian's Bower" lies 300 yards south-west of Alkborough church. A footpath leads to the site, located on high ground overlooking the confluence of the River Trent and the Humber estuary. Much speculation has centred upon the age and origin of the Julian's Bower; a date in the early 13th century is a popular choice. The maze is deeply sunk in a hollow, caused by many years of restoration, weed pulling and the removal of loose soil from the gulleys between the pathways. The oldest mention of it is to be found in the diary of Abraham de la Pryme, written between 1671 and 1704, where it is referred to as *"Gillian's Bore ... nothing but (a) great labarinth cut upon the ground with a hill cast up round about for the spectators to sit round about on to behold the sport"*. A note from 1866 records seeing villagers playing May-eve games on the maze *"under an indefinite persuasion of something unseen and unknown co-operating with them"*, a hint of traditional folk practices surviving at that time.

Tradition connects the maze with the nearby River Trent. The story tells of a river spirit known as Gur who took exception to the cutting of the turf maze on the hillside above his river and the visiting Christian pilgrims. To frighten the visitors to Jerusalem (as this maze was also called locally), he sent a great wave up the river in an attempt to wash the maze and the pilgrims away, but the effort was in vain, for the wave was not high enough to do any damage. He continues to try with each spring tide, when the Trent Bore (a small tidal wave) races up the river past Alkborough.

Alkborough Turf Maze

Badsell Park Farm - *"Golden Maze", Badsell Park Farm, Matfield, Tonbridge, Kent, TN12 7EW (tel. 0892 832549); golden leylandii hedge maze; 128 x 95 ft; planted 1991, to be opened 1993.*

Bath Festival Maze - *Beazer Gardens, near Pulteney Bridge, Bath, Avon, England (O.S. Ref. ST 753649); Bath stone maze paths in grass, elliptical, 97 x 73 ft; circular mosaic centrepiece depicting aspects of Bath, 15 x 15 ft; central mosaic designed by Randoll Coate; maze designed by Adrian Fisher of Minotaur Designs, 1984.*

"The Maze" was chosen as the theme for the 1984 Bath Festival, as expressed in music, opera, painting, sculpture, literature and film. It included a major exhibition of the work of the English sculptor and painter Michael Ayrton.

It was decided to build a full size permanent maze in the heart of the City of Bath, in the Beazer Gardens beside the River Avon, immediately below the Pulteney Bridge. Set in grass, the Bath stone paths describe an elegant ellipse, recalling the Georgian fanlights above the doors of Bath, the Brunel railway arches and the shape of the nearby Pulteney weir. Paradoxically the path to the goal is always shortened by taking turnings away from the centre. The maze can also be solved by going straight over each junction, when every path in the maze is walked once and once only.

At the centre is an Italian marble mosaic, fifteen feet in diameter, made up of over seventy-two thousand mosaic pieces in fifteen colours. It contains an enlarged representation of the famous Gorgon's Head of Bath, surrounded by six apses celebrating the four seasons, the four elements (Earth, Air, Fire and Water) and Bath's Celtic and Roman past. Its central circle ringed by six semi-circular apses echoes the central area in the labyrinth at Chartres Cathedral.

Each of these seven images are "Gaze-Mazes" in their own right - mazes solved by gazing rather than walking, each with a single line of coloured mosaic to follow. With allusions to Aridane's golden thread, the maze path around the Gorgon's head is depicted in gold Venetian glass. Persephone represents Bath, the City of Flowers, whilst Orpheus and his lyre emphasise the musical nature of the annual Bath Festival; Blalud's herd of swine in the magic mire represent Earth; the gaze-maze for Pegasus, representing Air, runs from mouth to eye; the Minotaur maze, for Fire, is traced from horn to horn; Dolphins, for Water, in white mosaic from tail to tail.

The Bath Festival Maze

The Central mosaic at Bath

Batheaston Church - *Batheaston, near Bath, Avon, England (O.S. Ref. ST 777679); copy of pavement maze formerly in Abbey of St Bertin at St Omer; stone pavement, square, 16ft 4in x 16ft 4in; built by Rev Paul Lucas, 1985.*

This is a replica of the unusual pavement labyrinth which formerly existed in the Abbey of St Bertin at St Omer, northern France. The Batheaston labyrinth is constructed of local stone flags set in the floor of the south aisle of the parish church. The maze paths are just wide enough to be walked. The design of this attractive labyrinth, and indeed of the original, is most unusual, being based upon the design of the Chartres labyrinth, but adapted almost beyond the point of recognition. The church is open at all reasonable times.

Batheaston Pavement Maze

Bicton Park Maze - *Bicton Park, Devon, England (tel. 0395 68465); upright wooden log maze in children's playground, in shape of giant footprint, 160 x 75 ft; designed by Adrian Fisher and Randoll Coate of Minotaur Designs, 1986.*

Blackgang Chine Maze - *Blackgang Chine, near Ventnor, Isle of Wight, England (tel. 0983 730330); privet hedges, rectangular, 84 x 75 ft; built by J Dabell, 1962.*

Blackpool Pleasure Beach Maze - *Blackpool Pleasure Beach, Lancashire, England (tel. 0253 41033); privet hedges, rectangular, 125 x 90 ft; built 1937; based on Hampton Court design.*

Blenheim Palace (1) - *Children's Colour Maze, Blenheim Palace, Woodstock, Oxfordshire, England (tel. 0993 811325); within walled garden; 'Minotaur Colour Maze' of interlocking plastic tiles, square, 25 x 25 ft; designed by Adrian Fisher of Minotaur Designs, 1991.*

Blenheim Palace (2) - *The Marlborough Maze, Blenheim Palace, Woodstock, Oxfordshire, England (tel. 0993 811325); design inspired by stone carvings on Palace by Grinling Gibbons; hedge maze with wooden bridges, and brick and stone pavilions, within walled garden; yew hedges, rectangular, 294 x 185 ft; designed by Adrian Fisher and Randoll Coate of Minotaur Designs, 1991; world's largest symbolic hedge maze.*

Blenheim Palace was given to the First Duke of Marlborough in recognition of his military victories of Blenheim, Malplaquet, Oudenard and Ramillies during the Marlborough Wars of 1704 - 1709. The palace was later the birthplace of Winston Churchill, Britain's greatest wartime leader of the twentieth century. The inspiration for the Marlborough Maze came from stone sculptures depicting the Panoply of Victory, carved by Grinling Gibbons for the roof of Blenheim Palace. Seen from above, the lines of the yew hedges portray pyramids of cannonballs, a cannon firing, and the air filled with banners, flags and the sound of trumpets. The maze has two entrances to left and right, with a central exit. The two wooden bridges create a three-dimensional puzzle, as well as giving tantalising views across parts of the world's largest symbolic hedge maze.

The Marlborough Maze, Blenheim Palace

Persephone

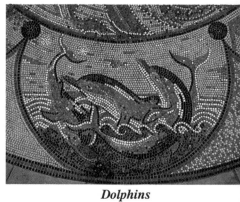

Dolphins

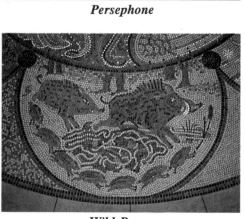

Wild Boars

Orpheus

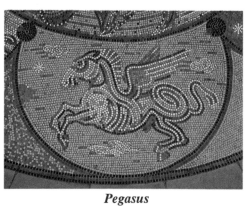

Pegasus

The Minotaur

The Bicton Maze

The Chatsworth Maze

Bodelwyddan Castle - *"The Thomas Mawson Maze", Bodelwyddan Castle, Bodelwyddan, Clwyd, LL18 5YA, Wales (tel. 0745 583539); hedge maze, Chamaecyparis lawsoniana 'Columnaris'; rectangular, approx. 82 x 82 ft; 1989.*

Boscastle - *Witches' House Museum, Boscastle, Cornwall, England; seven-ring Classical labyrinth, slate carving, 20 inches long.*

Two miles from Rocky Valley near Tintagel is the Witches' House Museum in Boscastle, where one of Britain's most fascinating labyrinths is displayed. In a case in the museum is a slate slab, approximately 20 inches long, which bears upon its upper face a carefully carved seven-circuit 'classical' labyrinth. A label attached to the stone simply states that is came from a farm at Michaelstow. The stone has had a long and complex history, having been passed down through successive generations of wise women or witches on the Isle of Man before coming to Cornwall. Its original purpose was as a divinatory tool, the user running a finger back and forth through the coils of the labyrinth to attain a state of intense concentration. The Witches' House is open during the summer months.

Bourn Church - *Bourn, Cambridgeshire, England (O.S. Ref. TL 325563); beneath west tower; design based on Hampton Court maze; pavement maze of black and red tiles, rectangular, 15 x 12 ft; 1875.*

This small tile labyrinth, in the parish church of St. Helena and St. Mary, was built in 1875, soon after the nearby Ely maze of 1870. As at Ely, the maze is also beneath the west tower, but the Bourn design is quite different, being a squared version of the Hampton Court hedge maze design. The font at the centre obscures part of the design, and was placed there at a later date. Open at all reasonable hours, by obtaining a key from a nearby house.

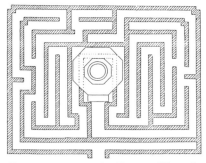

Pavement maze in Bourn Church

Breamore - *"Miz-Maze", Breamore Down, Breamore, Hampshire, England (O.S. Ref. SU 142203) (tel. 0725 22468); eleven-ring Medieval Christian design; turf maze, circular, 84 x 81 ft; presumed 13th century.*

Of all the surviving turf mazes in Europe, Breamore's Mizmaze is the unquestionably most exciting to discover, due to its remote location and intensely atmospheric situation in the middle of a wood.

Cut into the underlying chalk, the turf pathway has eleven circuits, with an 18 foot central mound. The trees of the encircling yew and hazel woodland grow right up to the outermost circuit, completely isolating this turf maze from the outside 20th century world, allowing a glimpse into the purpose of the medieval turf maze; this site has probably remained unchanged since its presumed 13th century construction.

Breamore Miz-Maze

Local tradition records that monks of Breamore Priory (now destroyed) once traversed the Mizmaze upon their knees to absolve their sins, possibly more for contemplative purposes than the penitential use suggested, and that a man could run from the Mizmaze to Gallows Hill and back (over a mile) in the time it took another to run the maze.

Finding this turf maze can be difficult, so use an O.S. map if possible; it is situated on a part of Breamore Down known locally as Mizmaze Hill, and can be approached either by a track leading from the A338 Salisbury road, or through the grounds of Breamore House (when open); ask for permission and directions first.

Bristol Roof Boss Maze, St Mary Redcliffe Church

Bristol Water Maze, Victoria Park

24 **British Maze Guide**

The Italianate Maze, Capel Manor

Flambards Colour Maze

Breamore Countryside Museum - *"Great British Maze",*
Breamore Countryside Museum, Breamore, Hampshire, England (tel.
0725 22468); in former walled garden of Breamore House; design
of four rotated five-bar gates; topiary "ewe" at centre; brick paths
in grass, square, 52 x 52 ft; design was winning entry of Sunday
Times 1984 maze design competition; designed by Ian Leitch, 1984.

Bristol Roof Boss Maze - *St Mary Redcliffe Church, Bristol,*
Avon, England (O.S. Ref. ST 591723); carved and gilded wooden
roof boss in north aisle; eleven-ring Medieval Christian design,
circular, 8 x 8 inches; fifteenth century.

This is not only one of the smallest, but also one of the most beautiful
labyrinths to be found in a British church. It takes the form of a
carved roof-boss, beautifully gilded and depicting an eleven-circuit
'Chartres-type' labyrinth. The roof-boss is only eight inches in
diameter, but is fairly easy to locate on the ceiling above the north
aisle (although there are over 1,200 bosses in the church!). This
would seem to be a unique example of its type and must date to the
mid-15th century when a major restoration of the church took place
after lightning felled the spire. The church is open to all reasonable
times and deserves some time to fully take in the fine Gothic
architecture and numerous interesting features.

Bristol Water Maze - *Victoria Park, Bristol, Avon, England*
(O.S. Ref. ST 595716); based on design of fifteenth century roof boss
in St Mary Redcliffe church nearby, to which this maze is aligned;
water maze in brick channel, circular, 25 x 25 ft; designed by Peter
Milner and Jane Norbury, 1984.

The course of the Bristol Water Maze is not a path but a brick
channel. Water wells up at the centre, and flows along every part of
its eleven rings. A twig or leaf can be slowly floated the entire
length, providing ample time for contemplation. Alternatively, the
visitor can trace the maze barefoot or in rubber boots. The design is
a copy of the roof-boss maze in St Mary Redcliffe Church. The
connection is emphasised by one axis of the maze pointing towards
the spire of St Mary Redcliffe Church, on the horizon a mile away.

Burford House Maze - *Burford House Gardens, Tenbury Wells, Hereford & Worcester, England (tel. 0584 810777); thuja plicata hedges; planted 1990, open 1992.*

Burt - *Labyrinth carvings and motifs, St Regnus' Church, Burt, County Donegal, Eire (Map Ref. C 365212); seven-ring Classical labyrinth design incorprating Christian cross, on doorhandles; also large labyrinth panel on outside wall; church consecrated in 1967.*

A number of labyrinths are incorporated within St. Regnus's Church at Burt, a small hamlet near Speenoge on the N13 road five miles northwest of Derry. The circular church, 103 feet in diameter with 13 foot thick walls, was modelled upon the Iron Age hill-fort of the Grianan of Aileach (map ref. C 368196) situated on an overlooking hill-top. All of the doors in the church have handles bearing a Classical labyrinth design, adapted slightly to emphasize the Christian cross inherent in the design. Outside stands a wall decorated with a number of moulded panels detailing the consecration of the church, with a large labyrinth panel set in the middle. The church, with its unique spire forming the entire roof, is well worth a visit.

Burton Agnes Hall Maze - *Burton Agnes Hall, Driffield, North Humberside (tel. 026 289 324); yew hedges and gravel paths, square, 100 x 100 ft; designed by Mrs Susan Cunliffe-Lister, 1990.*

Caerleon-on-Usk Legionary Museum - *Caerleon-on-Usk, Gwent, Wales (tel. 0633 432134); fine example of Roman mosaic labyrinth, in blue and white tesserae with additional red tesserae; square, 8 x 8 ft; second/third century.*

This Roman mosaic labyrinth was uncovered in 1865 at a depth of four feet in the north-east corner of the churchyard at Caerleon. The labyrinth was a three coil simple meander type, 8 feet square with a central compartment 16 inches square, which unfortunately was already damaged when found. Unusually, instead of decorating a villa, this labyrinth formed part of the floor of the principia, a room in the legionary fortress of Isca, and probably dates to the early years of the 3rd century AD. The mosaic is now in the Caerleon Museum.

Glendurgan Hedge Maze

The Archbishop's Maze, Greys Court

Hampton Court Palace hedge maze

Hilton turf maze

Capel Manor - *Italianate Maze, Capel Manor, Bullsmoor Lane, Enfield, Middlesex, England (tel. 0992 763849) (follow road directions from Junction 25 of M25); hedge maze in the spirit of the 'Italianate' gardening style, popular in England in the 1840s; central statuary, stone seating and illuminated fountains; holly hedges, oval, 121 x 88 ft; designed by Adrian Fisher of Minotaur Designs, 1991.*

The Italianate Maze forms one of a series of period gardens recreated at Capel Manor, and represents the nineteenth century. In England during the 1830s and 1840s, there was a craze for Italianate gardens. Several hedge mazes in the Italian style were planted, including one in Bridge End Gardens at Saffron Walden, and William Nesfield's designs at Somerleyton Hall, Worden Park, and South Kensington. Although this is not a direct copy of any single maze, the Capel Manor maze design brings together characteristic elements of the Italianate maze style; these include a neat perimeter with semicircular ends, each semicircle divided into four, a half-span shift in the central parallel section, and four delicate apses within the central goal. The substantial use of stonework completes its Italian character.

The Italianate Maze, Capel Manor

Cardiff Castle - *The Chaucer Room, Cardiff Castle, Cardiff, West Glamorgan, Wales (tel. 0222 822000); pavement labyrinth, in dark green and ivory white tiles; octagonal, 14 x 14 ft; designed by William Burges (1827-1881), built approximately 1875.*

The maze, partly overlapped by a fireplace, was built as part of Lord Bute's 19th century restoration of the castle. Its design is based on the pavement labyrinth in Amiens Cathedral. Regular daily tours.

Carnfunock Maze - *Carnfunock Amenity Park, near Larne, County Antrim, Northern Ireland (tel. 0574 70541); 3 miles north of Larne; hornbeam hedges, raised platform, 1991; open normal hours.*

Castle Bromwich Hall Gardens Maze - *Castle Bromwich Hall Gardens, West Midlands, England (tel. 021 749 4100); restored with holly and hawthorn hedges (originally just holly), rectangular mirror image of Hampton Court design, 76 x 23 ft (paths 18", beds 36"); just possibly part of 1730s garden; most probably built by Lady Ida Bridgeman in late 19th century; restored by Martin Locock, 1990.*

Cawdor Maze - *Cawdor Castle, near Inverness, Nairnshire, Scotland (O.S. Ref. NH 847498) (tel. 06677 615); in walled garden; square hedge maze, without junctions; planted 1981, open 1994.* **Please Note - this maze is not open to the public until 1994.**

This unicursal hedge maze, in the former wall garden, derives its design from the ancient Roman mosaic maze at Coimbra in Portugal.

Chatsworth Maze - *Chatsworth House, Baslow, near Bakewell, Derbyshire, England (OS Ref. SK 263697) (tel. 024 688 2204); on former site of Paxton's Great Conservatory; yew hedges, rectangular, 130 x 115 ft; planted by D. A. Fisher, 1962.* **Please Note - the maze itself is not open to the public, although visitors may walk round its perimeter, and admire it from surrounding vantage points.**

The Chatsworth maze has one of the most magnificent settings of any hedge maze in the world. Although planted in 1962, it uses an earlier maze design, and occupies the former site of Paxton's Great Stove glasshouse. The maze is surrounded by mature Wellingtonias, raised grass banks and paths on all sides, and stone bridges at each end. The Chatworth maze acts like a "magnet" in the landscape, drawing visitors through various parts of the gardens before they reach the maze.

Hever Castle hedge maze

Tudor Rose Maze, Kentwell Hall

Chenies Hedge Maze - *Chenies Manor House, Chenies, Buckinghamshire, England (tel. 0494 2888); maze design derived from mathematical "net" of 20-faced Icosahedron; yew hedges, rectangular, 66 x 60 ft; maze designed by Jeremy Prosser; centrepiece designed by Caroline Ray; both being winning entries of Sunday Times "Year of the Maze" Design Competition; 1991.*

Chenies Turf Maze - *Chenies Manor House, Chenies, Buckinghamshire, England (tel. 0494 2888); maze design based on portrait of Edward, Lord Russell, dated 1573, now hanging in Woburn Abbey, Bedfordshire; maze of gravel paths in grass, circular, 48 x 48 ft; built by Denys Tweddell, 1983.*

This elegantly spiralling design is based on the depiction of an ornamental maze in the background of a painting of Edward, Lord Russell, the grandson of the first Earl of Bedford, who owned Chenies in the mid-16th century. The painting is dated 1573; this modern maze may thus provide an accurate replica of a 16th century garden maze. Open Wednesdays & Thurdays, 2-5pm, April-October.

Compton - *Watts Mortuary Chapel, Compton, Surrey, England (O.S. Ref. SU 956474); corbels of four angels holding labyrinths, and a fifth gilded labyrinth incorporated within altar; built 1896.*

The Watts Mortuary Chapel stands in Compton village cemetery on a small hill. On its outer walls, beneath terracotta panels of art nouveau angels and celtic interlace, twelve corbels of robed angels bear circular shields representing the Truth, the Way and the Life; four of the angels support seven-ring labyrinths which represent the Way. Inside, the chapel is richly decorated, and the altar bears a gilded labyrinth (based on the pavement labyrinth at San Vitale, Ravenna, Italy) supported by winged angels. This curious yet outrageously beautiful chapel was built between 1896 and the early 1900's by Mary Watts in memory of her father, George Frederic Watts, the Victorian artist and sculptor. Open daily until dusk.

Consett - *"The Jolly Drovers Maze", Consett and Sunderland Railway Path, Jolly Drovers Roundabout, Leadgate, near Consett, County Durham, England (OS Ref. NZ 133519) (tel. "Sustrans" office, 0207 281259); giant earth maze on site of former colliery, approx. 2 acres, designed by Andy Goldsworthy, 1989.*

Crawley - *County Mall, Crawley, West Sussex; two pavement tile mazes - a Minotaur colour maze, and a double puzzle maze (inspired by Escher) with mosaic centrepiece; both rectangular; 22 x 18 ft and 32 x 12 ft; designed by Adrian Fisher of Minotaur Designs, 1992.*

The colour maze resembles the game of Hopscotch, though its puzzle is nothing like so obvious. The double puzzle maze, inspired by Escher's drawings, paradoxically offers two mutually exclusive paths.

Crystal Palace Maze - *Crystal Palace Park, Crystal Palace Park Road, Bromley, Kent (tel. 081 313 4426); hornbeam hedge maze with gravel paths; circular, 160 x 160 ft; planted c. 1865; restored by Patrick Phillips, of London Borough of Bromley, 1988.*

Dalby - *"City of Troy", near Dalby, North Yorkshire, England (O.S. Ref. SE 626719); between villages of Dalby and Brandsby; seven-ring Classical design; turf path, circular, 26 x 22 ft; beside road, enclosed by low white fencing; date unknown.*

The smallest surviving turf maze in Europe, and the only remaining example in Yorkshire, lies beside a minor road between Brandsby and Dalby. It is notoriously difficult to find; take the B1363 road northeast out of Brandsby, to a crossroads; turn right along the road to Dalby and Terrington, and then turn sharp left which leads ESE for a mile or so; just past a wood on the south side of the road, the maze is surrounded by a low white wooden railing on the north verge.

The location of this "City of Troy" is one of the most evocative of all labyrinth sites in the British Isles. Set high on the Howardian Hills, York Minster 13 miles to the south can be clearly seen on a fine day. The seven paths that encircle the central goal are banked towards the centre which allows for easy running, although the total exercise only takes a couple of minutes; traditionally, running the maze more than nine times will result in bad luck. There is a long tradition of cutting and caring for a turf maze here; an earlier re-cutting in 1860 was aided by a plan carved on a barn door at nearby Skewsby (now sadly lost), continuing a tradition which despite minor movements of the exact site has possibly continued for a thousand years or more.

Dart Valley Railway Maze - *Dart Valley Railway, Buckfastleigh, Devon, England (tel. 0364 42338); Cupressus leylandii hedges, rectangular; planted 1986.*

Doddington Hall Maze - *Doddington Hall, Doddington, Lincolnshire (O.S. Ref. SK 900697) (tel. 0522 694308); gravel paths in grass, circular, 75 x 75 ft; designed by Anthony Jarvis, 1985.*

Drusilla's Zoo Park - *Children's Colour Maze, Drusilla's Zoo Park, Alfriston, East Sussex (tel. 0323 870234); outdoor 'Minotaur Colour Maze' of interlocking plastic tiles, square, 25 x 25 ft; designed by Adrian Fisher of Minotaur Designs, 1991.*

Ely Cathedral Maze - *Ely Cathedral, Ely, Cambridgeshire, England (O.S. Ref. TL 541803) (tel. 0353 667735); maze path length is same as height of west tower, beneath which it is situated; black and white stone pavement maze, square, 20 x 20 ft; designed by Sir Gilbert Scott, 1870.*

Ely has the only pavement labyrinth of any British cathedral. This delightful Victorian example was built by Sir Gilbert Scott during his restoration work on the cathedral. The labyrinth, picked out in black and white stone, lies just inside the doors under the west tower and has a path length of 215 feet, precisely the height of the tower directly above it. The design of the labyrinth is unusual, since it does not possess the internal rotational symmetry characteristic of Medieval Christian labyrinths. The Cathedral is renowned for its architecture, wooden octagonal lantern tower and stained glass windows, and is open during standard hours; an admission fee is charged.

Flambards Theme Park - *Children's Colour Maze, Flambards Theme Park, Helston, Cornwall, England (tel. 0326 574549); outdoor 'Minotaur Colour Maze' of interlocking plastic tiles, square, 25 x 25 ft; designed by Adrian Fisher of Minotaur Designs, 1991.*

Like any puzzle maze, this Colour Maze has junctions connected by paths. However, you must change the colour of your path, every time you reach a junction square. This maze is great fun to solve.

Glastonbury Tor Maze - *Glastonbury, Somerset. Seven-ring labyrinth footpath along grass terraces to summit; identified in 1979.*

This is one of the most controversial mazes in Britain - not least, is it a true maze at all? Normally a maze or labyrinth is a deliberately man-made artefact, carefully and completely designed before it is built. Undeniably, the broad man-made terraces on Glastonbury Tor were created many centuries ago. Yet the first time it was suggested that they formed a seven-ring Classical labyrinth was in 1969 by Geoffrey Russell. In 1979, Geoffrey Ashe published a suggested plan of the maze; despite best endeavours, it is clear that the maze path is not a properly-designed "fit" (as should be the case if the terraces had been originally designed as a labyrinth). Whatever the truth of its origins as a maze, the Tor is a hauntingly beautiful place to visit.

Glendurgan Maze - *Glendurgan House, near Falmouth, Cornwall (OS Ref. SW 772277) (tel. National Trust Regional Office, 0208 74281); laurel hedges, 133 x 108 ft; designed by Alfred Fox, 1833.*

The Glendurgan maze, created by Alfred Fox in 1833, is among Britain's earliest surviving hedge mazes. It is one of three mazes owned by the National Trust, the other two being at Greys Court and Tatton Park.

Plan of the Glendurgan Maze

Glendurgan's free-flowing design was derived from the design of the hedge maze that formerly existed in the Sydney Gardens, Bath, between 1804 and 1840. Its inspired position on one side of the narrow valley gives an almost bird's eye view of its sinuous laurel hedges from the opposite side.

Greys Court - *"The Archbishop's Maze", Greys Court, near Henley-on-Thames, Oxfordshire, England (O.S. Ref. SU 725834) (tel. 04917 529); owned by National Trust; brick paths in grass maze, with central sundial on inscribed pillar and two stone pavement crosses; circular, 85 x 85 ft; designed by Adrian Fisher and Randoll Coate of Minotaur Designs; dedicated by Dr Robert Runcie, Archbishop of Canterbury, 24th October 1981.*

In his enthronement address (25th March, 1980), Archbishop Runcie spoke of a maze: *"I had a dream of a maze. There were some people very close to the centre, but they could not find a way through. Just outside the maze others were standing. They were further away from the heart of the maze, but they would be there sooner than the party that fretted and fumed inside."*

The building of a maze in response to this sermon was Lady Brunner's inspired idea. The maze abounds in Christian symbolism: its cruciform shape, image of the Crown of Thorns, seven days of Creation, nine hours of Agony and twelve Apostles. At the centre, a simple Roman cross of Bath stone is laid within an elaborate Byzantine cross of blue Westmorland stone. These proclaim the reconciliation between East and West, Catholic and Protestant, Roman and Orthodox - a vital aspect of Robert Runcie's life work. In one sense, the maze is a puzzle, and there are various junctions with choices to be made. However, by crossing straight over each diamond-shaped thorn, one walks the entire quarter mile path of the maze. This route represents the Christian Path of Life.

Just before reaching the centre, the path goes past the diamond-shaped inscription: *"This maze was dedicated by Robert Runcie, Archbishop of Canterbury, 24th October 1981."* At the centre an armillary sundial is supported by a stone pillar, inscribed with lines from Saint Augustine, Julian of Norwich, Siegfried Sassoon and Robert Gittings.

Hadstock Churchyard - *Hadstock, Essex, England (OS Ref. TL 559448); in north-east of churchyard, on left side of path; 18 inch wide bronze replica of Arkville labyrinth, on gravestone of Michael Ayrton, who died in 1975.*

This simple stone slab is situated in the north-east side of the graveyard, to the left of the path leading up to the church. It bears no inscription, just a bronze copy of the Arkville Maze, New York State, USA; for this is the tomb of Michael Ayrton (1921-1975), designer of mazes (including the Arkville Maze), sculptor and writer of the novel "The Maze Maker", a life of Daedalus.

Maze at Hadstock

Hampton Court Maze - *Hampton Court Palace, East Molesey, Surrey, England (tel. 081 977 8441); yew hedges, trapezoid shape, 222 x 82 ft; designed by George London and Henry Wise, c.1690; Britain's oldest surviving hedge maze.*

Hampton Court Palace has probably the world's most famous hedge maze. It was planted as part of the gardens laid out for William of Orange between 1689 and 1695, by George London and Henry Wise. Its unusual trapezoid shape is explained by the plan of the Wilderness, where the shape of the maze is dictated by two diagonal paths and a further curving path. This helps date the maze since clearly the maze could not have been planted prior to the layout of the Wilderness.

Early on, the maze faced its gravest challenge when Capability Brown became the Royal Gardener, and for twenty years lived in the house alongside the maze. Brown's reputation had been established by sweeping away some two hundred fine gardens all over the country, but the king expressly ordered Brown not to interfere with it.

The Hampton Court Maze was described in Jerome K. Jerome's "Three Men in a Boat", and this novel established in many minds the connection between mazes, blazers and straw boater hats. Since early Victorian times, this maze design has been copied over a dozen times in Britain, North America and Australia; such was its reputation, that others were keen to emulate it when creating a hedge maze elsewhere. The Hampton Court maze continues to attract hundreds of thousands of visitors each year, and remains in many ways synonymous with hedge mazes throughout the English speaking world.

Plan of the Hampton Court Maze

Hatfield House - *Low Box Maze, Hatfield House, Hatfield, Hertfordshire, England (tel. 0707 262823); low box hedges with gravel paths, square, 31 x 31 ft; in front of Old Palace, to be observed only, not walked in; designed by Lady Salisbury, 1980s.*

Hatfield House has two fine mazes, although neither is open to the public. The full-height yew hedge maze was planted in 1840, and is thought to replace an even earlier one. The hedges of the smaller maze are only a few inches high, in the parterre style. Planted in Buxus sempervirens, it is part of Lady Salisbury's design for a Tudor garden in front of the Old Palace. The popular misconception that mazes are often made of box probably arises from the rectangular clipped shapes of a hedge maze, which appear to be box-shaped.

Hereford Cathedral - *Mappa Mundi, Hereford Cathedral, Hereford & Worcester, England (O.S. Ref. SO 510398); the Mappa Mundi was drawn by Richard de Bello c. 1280 AD, and brought to Hereford in 1305; size of whole map is 1.65 x 1.34 m., 5 x 4 ft; the map depicts a labyrinth on the island of Crete, although its design is of an eleven-ring Medieval Christian labyrinth.*

The legendary Cretan Labyrinth is depicted on the Hereford Mappa Mundi, an early medieval map of the world, completed c.1280 by Richard de Bello and brought by him in 1305 to Hereford Cathedral where it hangs to this day. The map of the world, worked in inks and pigments on vellum, is 52 inches in diameter and shows a surprisingly accurate, albeit curiously shaped, view of Europe, Africa and Asia with many factual and mythological beasts depicted, including the surprising appearance of the Minotaur somewhat far from home in Scythia. The Mappa Mundi is kept in the Cathedral Treasury, open 10am to 5pm daily; an admission fee is charged.

Hever Castle Maze - *Hever Castle, Edenbridge, Kent, England (tel. 0732 865224); hedge maze installed to recreate Tudor atmosphere, at castle where Henry VIII courted Anne Boleyn; yew hedges, square, 75 x 75 ft; built by William Waldorf Astor, 1905.*

Henry VIII came to Hever Castle to court Anne Boleyn, the home of Anne Boleyn's family from 1462 until 1538. The castle dates back to thirteenth century. Its final historical twist came in 1903, when William Waldorf Astor, the American millionaire, bought the castle. In his grand scheme, he added a "Tudor" village and a unique Italian garden, to accommodate his extensive collection of statuary and antiquities. The yew maze and a set of topiary chessmen were laid out between the two moats to recreate a Tudor atmosphere. The combination of moats, yew hedges, and a classic medieval castle makes Hever Castle a sensational period landscape.

Hilton Maze - *The Common, Hilton, Cambridgeshire, England (O.S. Ref. TL 293663); originally eleven-ring Medieval Christian design, now with only nine rings of paths; turf path, circular, 55 x 55 ft; central 8 ft high stone pillar dated 1660.*

Hilton Green is reputed to have been landscaped in the 18th century by Capability Brown who had a house at nearby Fenstanton, which would have involved him in restoring the turf maze; he clearly took less exception to this than most of the hedge mazes he encountered! The present design is a nine-ring variant of the usual eleven-ring Medieval Christian design, which has evolved through inaccuracies made when cutting and trimming the turf circuits over the years. The central pillar states (in Latin): *"William Sparrow, born 1641, died at the age of 88, formed these circuits in 1660"*. This would seem to date the maze to 1660, but it has been conjectured that William Sparrow, at the age of 19, had possibly only restored an earlier overgrown turf maze. 1660 was the year of the restoration of the monarchy under Charles II and the collapse of the Puritan-dominated Commonwealth (1649-1659), during which many traditional customs and dances had been outlawed, and many turf mazes would have fallen into disrepair. The maze is open at all times.

Hollywood Stone - *National Museum, Kildare Street, Dublin, Eire; seven-ring "Classical" labyrinth, 30 x 30 inches; found 1911, moved to National Museum 1925; probable date c. 550 AD.*

The Hollywood Stone

The Hollywood Stone was found by chance when a group of people chasing a stoat turned over a large boulder under which the animal had hidden. The base of the stone bore a large carving of a seven-ring Classical labyrinth, 30 inches in diameter.

The Hollywood stone was removed to the National Museum in 1925, where it has been labelled "Neolithic, c.2000 BC". The spot where the stone was found is beside a trackway known as "St. Kevin's Road", which leads from Hollywood to the famous 6th century Christian foundation of Glendalough, and the stone may have served some purpose in guiding pilgrims along the path to Glendalough. This would suggest that the true age of the Hollywood labyrinth is more likely to be c. 550 AD.

Hull City Hall - *Hull, North Humberside, England; Roman mosaic labyrinth, excavated from Roman Villa at Harpham, Yorkshire in 1904; square, 11 x 11 ft; early 4th century AD.* **Please Note - this labyrinth is currently not on view, although it is hoped that it will be put on public display again, sometime in the future.**

The design of this labyrinth was commonly used by Roman artisans in mosaics throughout the Roman Empire, with the small central compartment occupied by a flower with four petals. This mosaic is dated as early 4th century, since an unworn coin of 304 AD was found below another mosaic in a nearby room. The labyrinth design as known today contains an error almost certainly not present when originally laid in the early 4th century.

Hull Pavement Maze - *King Edward Street, Hull, North Humberside, England; eleven-ring Medieval Christian design; red and buff brick pavement; square, 43ft 3in x 43ft 3in; built by Philip Heselton, 1987.*

This design of this labyrinth in Hull city centre is similar to that of Julian's Bower turf maze at nearby Alkborough, but adapted into a square shape. Its central plaque is inscribed: *"This pavement maze is built to traditional principles, having no dead ends, only a single path leading eventually to the centre. In medieval times mazes were run or danced round on festive occasions. Hull City Council 1987".*

Irvine Beach Maze - *Irvine Beach Park, Irvine New Town, Ayrshire, Scotland; concrete paths in grass, circular, 108 x 108 ft; 1980s.*

Irvine Town Centre Maze - *Irvine New Town, Ayrshire, Scotland; stained glass window, circular, 5 x 5 ft; 1980s.*

This brightly-coloured stained glass maze window is in the shopping mall at Irvine town centre. There is also a small maze in relief on the wall opposite.

Itchen Stoke - *St Mary's Church, Itchen Stoke, Hampshire, England (O.S. Ref SU 559324); pavement maze beneath altar, in russett and green tiles; circular, 15 x 15 ft; c.1866.*

St. Mary's lies on the B3047 road between Winchester and Alresford. Built on the site of an earlier foundation, the architect, Henry Conybeare, modelled the church on Sainte Chapelle in Paris. The maze design is a scaled down copy of the pavement labyrinth in Chartres Cathedral, France. The pavement maze tiles are partially covered by the altar; too small to walk, this attractive maze was clearly designed for symbolic rather than practical purposes. The church is cared for by the Redundant Churches Fund, and is open at all reasonable hours; a key is available at a nearby house.

Kentwell Hall - *Tudor Rose Maze, Kentwell Hall, Long Melford, Suffolk, England (O.S. Ref. TL 863479) (tel. 0787 310207); brick mosaic pavement maze, circular, 70 x 70 ft; brick diamond details designed by Randoll Coate; maze design by Adrian Fisher of Minotaur Designs; opened 1985; world's largest brick pavement maze; winner of British Tourist Authority's 1984 "Heritage in the Making" Award.*

Filling the main courtyard of moated Kentwell Hall, the Tudor Rose Maze was built with twenty-seven thousand red and white paving bricks. Set in the design are fifteen diamonds of etched brick, decorated with symbols representing the Tudor dynasty.

The maze design simultaneously offers a five-fold unicursal labyrinth, a maze puzzle, and at the centre a giant chess board. The five separate progressions through the maze, from the five outer thorns to the centre, echo the internal rotational symmetry hidden within

Classical and Medieval Christian labyrinths. Alternatively, the rose becomes a three-dimensional puzzle maze, by observing junctions and flyovers indicated by the brick paths. This unique combination of entertainments in the pattern of the Tudor Rose was built to celebrate five hundred years since the start of the Tudor dynasty in 1485.

Landmark Maze - *Landmark Centre, near Carrbridge, Inverness-shire, Scotland (tel. 047 984 613); raised wooden paths in woodland; built c. 1978.*

Lappa Valley Railway - *Lappa Maze, Lappa Valley Railway, St Newlyn East, Cornwall, England (OS Ref. SW 839558) (tel. 087 251 317); 3 miles from Newquay; brick paths in grass, in the shape of Trevithick's steam locomotive, 161 x 101 ft; designed by Adrian Fisher and Randoll Coate of Minotaur Designs, 1982.*

The Lappa Maze represents the world's first locomotive, built by the Cornish inventor Trevithick. His historic engine predated the more famous ones built by the Stephensons, such as "Locomotion" and "Rocket". The brick paths portray Trevithick's 1804 Tramroad Locomotive, with its vast flywheel and interacting pattern of cogs, to a scale of eight times the size of the original engine. The centre of the small driving cog is the goal, reached by following the huge connecting rod from the pistons. On the driving wheels, visitors turn tightly to and fro between the meshing cogs; on the immense flywheel, children can run in imitation of the whirling speed of its circumference. Hidden within the design are the giant letters "T" for Trevithick and "L" for Lappa; the date of Trevithick's Locomotive, 1804, expressed in Roman figures, "MDCCCIIII"; and "E.W.R." for the East Wheal Rose Mine, beside which the maze is sited.

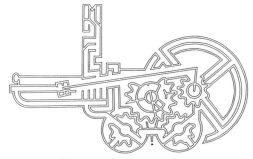

Plan of the Lappa Maze

Leeds Castle Maze - *Leeds Castle, near Maidstone, Kent, England (tel. 0622 765400); 5 miles east of Maidstone; yew hedge maze, with central stone tower, underground grotto decorated with seashells, statues and fountains, and 90 ft exit tunnel; square, 156 x 156 ft; maze designed by Adrian Fisher and Randoll Coate of Minotaur Designs, and Vernon Gibberd, 1988; grotto designed and created by Vernon Gibberd, Simon Verity and Diana Reynell; winner of 1988 Regional Award of the Royal Institute of British Architects.*

Leeds Castle, described by Lord Conway as "the loveliest castle in the world", is set on two Kentish lake islands. A ninth-century thane named Ledian originally erected a wooden fortress on the site. Queen Eleanor, wife of Edward I, was the first of several Queens of England to live there. In 1974 Lady Baillie, the last private owner, set up a charitable trust to maintain the castle for the nation and for the enjoyment of all, to assist Medicine, and to encourage the Arts.

The formal hedge maze, opened on 25th May 1988 by Princess Alexandra, tempts visitors beyond the Culpeper Gardens and the Aviary. The maze is a topiary castle with castellated yew hedges, an entrance bridge and a central tower. Inside, the maze puzzle is challenging and teasing in several ways. From its central raised goal, the view from its stone parapet rewards the visitor with images of a Queen's crown and a chalice, both laid out in the rows of the hedges.

Looking down, visitors see splashing water and light twenty feet below them. Beneath the stone tower, they discover the entrance to an underground grotto decorated with thousands of sea shells, with statues in niches, and water cascading over a grotesque face in the manner of the Bomarzo giants in Italy. Still deeper, a ninety foot underground passage beneath the hedges of the maze leads through a dramatic vortex, confronting visitors with a flooded cave, the seat of the nymph of the grotto, before they ascend to the outside world.

Leicester University - *"Mathematica" Colour Maze, outside the Mathematics Building, Leicester University, Leicester, England; brick pavement 'colour maze', in five colours of paving brick; square, 20 x 20 ft; designed by Adrian Fisher of Minotaur Designs, 1991.*

Minotaur Colour Mazes were conceived by Adrian Fisher, and first published in Scientific American in December 1986. Mathematically, colour mazes are surprisingly difficult to solve, and contain elements of topology, puzzles and logic.

All mazes consist of nodes which are junctions or decision points, and paths. The nodes in this colour maze are russet brick squares, connected by paths of red, buff and brown bricks. The rule is to change path colour each time a node is reached in the repeated sequence Red-Brown-Buff. From a starting point on the first Red path, the goal is the centre square. A second way to tackle the maze is to follow the sequence Red-Buff-Brown. Each square is indicated by a different letter of the alphabet, to chart progress. Analytical methods can be used to demonstrate the shortest solution in each of the two sequences. Incidentally, one part of the lettering can also be followed to spell the word MATHEMATICA, but this has nothing to do with the puzzle.

This maze was designed by Adrian Fisher in memory of his sister Victoria Fisher, who was a Lecturer in Law at the University from 1979 to 1986.

Leighton Hall Maze - *The Caterpillar Maze, Leighton Hall, Carnforth, Lancashire, England (tel. 0524 734474); gravel paths in grass; built by Mr and Mrs R G Reynolds, 1990.*

Longleat Maze - *Longleat House, near Warminster, Wiltshire (tel. 098 53 551); yew hedges and wooden bridges, rectangular, 380 x 175 ft; designed by Greg Bright, 1978; world's largest hedge maze.*

Lord Weymouth wanted to create a hedge maze on a scale in keeping with this famous Elizabethan house; the world's largest hedge maze was the result. The maze contains various innovative puzzle features.

Six bridges create a three-dimensional puzzle. Spiral junctions are intended to add confusion by repetition. Elongated fork junctions are cunningly used, since visitors are thought to prefer to 'conserve their momentum' instead of making U turns. The whirling lines and the lack of any rectangular grid add further disorientation. Allow an hour and a half to solve this maze!

Machynlleth - *"Environmental Maze", National Centre for Alternative Technology, Llwyngwern Quarry, Machynlleth, Powys, Wales (tel. 0654 702400); the maze choices simulate government environmental decision-making; rhododendron, birch and oak hedges; designed by Pat Borer, 1980.*

Manningford Nurseries - *"The Manningford Maze", Manningford Nurseries, Manningford Abbots, Wiltshire, England (tel. 0672 62232); low box hedges with grass paths; trapezoid shape, 109 x 85 ft; designed by Adrian Fisher and Lesley Beck of Minotaur Designs, 1991.*

The design of the Manningford Maze was derived from a square 17th century knot garden design, which has been transformed into a puzzle maze. Its trapezoid shape gives the design added vigour.

Plan of the Manningford Maze

Margam Park Maze - *Margam Country Park, Port Talbot, West Glamorgan, Wales (tel. 0639 881635); Cupressus leylandii hedges, rectangular, 198 x 189 ft; built by Dr Terence Stevens, 1986.*

The largest hedge maze in Wales lies within an old walled garden, with a heart of flowers at its goal. One-way wooden doors in the perimeter provide emergency exits. Unfortunately the distinctly sloping site makes this maze unsuitable for those in wheelchairs.

Mayflower Park Maze - *Mayflower Park, Southampton, Hampshire, England; small maze of low concrete walls in children's playground, hexagonal; built in the 1980s.*

Merritown House - *Alice-in-Wonderland Maze, Merritown House, Hurn, near Christchurch, Dorset, England (tel. 0202 483004) (road entrance on southern side of Hurn Airport); hedge maze with wooden bridge and central mound; portrays various characters and creatures from story of Alice-in-Wonderland; beech hedges, octagonal, 240 x 240 ft; designed by Adrian Fisher and Randoll Coate of Minotaur Designs, 1991.*

The Alice-in-Wonderland maze is the centrepiece of a new seven acre garden which Russell Lucas-Rowe is creating. Set amidst avenues of topiary and entered under a viewing bridge, this beech maze contains gigantic shapes within its hedges. In this topsy-turvy dream world, none of the images are the same way up, but they are all the right way up when seen from the top of the central mound. Rotating clockwise, the principal characters in the story are portrayed - Alice, Mad Hatter, White Rabbit, Cheshire Cat, Queen of Hearts, Gryffon, Mock Turtle and Dodo. The centre of the maze portrays the White Rabbit's pocket watch, with steps up and down the mound indicating four o'clock, perpetual tea-time. The central octagon is also the body of a giant tea-pot, with the Dormouse sleeping in its handle. Finally, along a short exit, visitors leave the maze just like the ending of Alice's dream, in a flurry of playing cards.

OPPOSITE *"Mathematica" brick pavement colour maze, Leicester University*

Milton Keynes - *Willen Maze, Willen Lake, Milton Keynes, Buckinghamshire, England (O.S. Ref. SP 880405); near the Peace Pagoda; gravel paths in grass, circular with bastions, 345 x 345 ft; design is enlarged copy of Saffron Walden; built 1984.*

One of the strangest of modern labyrinths, it is formed by a gravel pathway set into turf, and is one of the largest labyrinths in Britain. The design is a slightly adapted copy of the largest surviving ancient turf labyrinth at Saffron Walden, but at about three times the scale, thus producing a path over two miles long. Those prepared for the challenge can find the maze near the Peace Pagoda, an easy walk from the car park; the maze is freely open at all times. There are several other mazes in Milton Keynes, but this is the largest.

Mistley Place Maze - *Mistley Place, Manningtree, Essex, England (tel. 0206 396483); beech hedges, planted c. 1870 (or 1890?); replanted in holly by Frank Pearson, 1989.* **Please Note - this maze is growing, following restoration, so its condition is not yet pristine.**

Newquay Zoo - *Dragon Maze, Newquay Zoo, Newquay, Cornwall, England (tel. 0637 873342); Eleagnus hedges, 210 x 85 ft; designed by Adrian Fisher and Randoll Coate of Minotaur Designs, 1984.*

Mythical creatures are often feared within labyrinths, but here the beast is the labyrinth itself. One can imagine this menacing creature occupying the nearby St Michael's Mount until the advent of Christianity, when life got too hot for dragons. Whatever his misty past, the zoo keepers found a safe paddock all for himself. Since this is Cornwall, he enjoys the protection of the Duke of Cornwall, the Heir Apparent, and so wears about his neck an heraldic collar, the label of three points.

Plan of the Dragon Maze

Parham Park - *"Veronica's Maze", Parham Park, near Pulborough, West Sussex, England (tel. 0903 742021); unusual one-way maze puzzle; brick paths in grass, 96 x 60 ft; designed by Adrian Fisher and Lesley Beck of Minotaur Designs, 1991.*

This maze with its quarter mile of brick paths was built on the lawn where the owner Veronica Tritton used to play as a girl. Nowhere in the design is there a straight line, since the design was inspired by ancient embroidery over the Great Bed within the house. This is a completely new form of maze puzzle, with just one extra rule: you must not turn back on yourself, once you have started walking.

Plan of Veronica's Maze

Paultons Park - *"The Clock Maze", Paultons Park, Ower, near Romsey, Hampshire, England (tel. 0703 813025); hedge maze with ornate central clock; square, 100 x 100 ft; designed by John Mancey, 1991.*

Pennard Maze - *Three Cliffs Bay, Pennard, Gower Peninsula, West Glamorgan, Wales (O.S. Ref. SS 539882); seven-ring Classical labyrinth design; stone-lined paths in grass, roughly circular, 31 x 29 ft; built by Joe, a visitor from Poland, 1972.*

The maze is situated on the flats behind a shingle bar across the Pennard Pill, although it is best approached from Southgate, across the golf course. Despite its modern origin, the labyrinth is already known amongst local children as 'The Faerie Ring' and receives regular visits and maintenance from local people and holidaymakers alike. The fact that it has survived this long bodes well for its future; the path followed by countless feet between the stone walls is deeply worn into the soft ground, and no doubt in years to come its already 'ancient' appearance will confuse many researchers and visitors.

The Grotto, Leeds Castle Maze

The hedge maze, Longleat House

Tapestry of the "Alice-in-Wonderland" Maze, Merritown House

"Veronica's Maze", Parham Park

Ragley Hall - *Snakes and Ladders Maze, Ragley Hall, Alcester, Warwickshire, England (tel. 0789 762009); tall concrete walls, on two levels, rectangular; originally built by Maurice Rich, c. 1980.*

Rathmore Maze - *Rathmore, ruined church of St. Lawrence, Rathmore, County Meath, Republic of Ireland (N 753670); eleven-ring Medieval Christian labyrinth design; circular, 14 x 14 inches; mid-fifteenth century; found in 1931 during restoration work.*

The labyrinth is carved on a block of stone which may formerly have served as a corbel or as part of a memorial or tombstone. The carving was found during restoration work on the church, buried among debris on the floor, and presumably dates to the mid-fifteenth century, when Sir Thomas Plunkett commissioned the building of the church. The carved stone is now attached to the inside of the south wall. The church is located in a field to the north of the L21/N51 Naven and Athboy road, 3 miles NE of Athboy. A signposted footpath leads to the church.

Rhinefield Maze - *Rhinefield House Hotel, near Brockenhurst, Hampshire, England (tel. 0590 22922); design based on Hampton Court maze; yew hedges, rectangular, 135 x 69 ft (41 x 21 m.); originally built 1890, restored by Kim Wilkie, 1990.*

Rhinefield House is now a hotel; maze visitors are invited to patronise the hotel, if they wish to see the maze and other parts of the newly-restored gardens.

Rocky Valley Carvings - *Rocky Valley, near Tintagel, Cornwall, England (OS Ref. SX 073893); two rock carvings, circular; 9 x 9 inches, and 9 x 7 inches; dates not known.*

Two labyrinths are carved on a rockface in Rocky Valley, north of the B3263 road, one mile north-east of Tintagel. To find the carvings, park in the lay-by opposite the Trevillett Mill trout farm entrance, and follow the footpath (slippery when wet) past the mill on the right-hand bank of the stream until a ruined mill building is reached. Behind the building is a vertical rockface upon which are carved two seven-circuit Classical labyrinths, both nine inches wide. The official sign mounted on the rockface states that the carvings date to the "Bronze Age, 1800-1400 BC", although this dating is suspect. Two plausible dates have been suggested: firstly that they date from the early 6th century when an early Christian missionary, St. Nectan, occupied a cell higher up the valley; and secondly that they only date to the late 17th century, being contemporary with the now ruined mill. Rocky Valley is open to the public at all times.

Russborough Maze - *Russborough House, Blessington, County Wicklow, Republic of Ireland (tel. 353 45 65301); statue of Cupid on central pillar; beech hedge maze, square, 142 x 142 ft; designed by Adrian Fisher and Randoll Coate of Minotaur Designs, 1993.*

Plan of the Russborough Maze

The only entrance and exit to the Russborough Maze is through the eighteenth-century riding school. The design of this formal hedge maze, planted in 1989, conceals a clue to the identity of its owner, since Sir Alfred Beit's family were early pioneers in the world diamond industry. A statue of Cupid stands on a column at the centre, tantalisingly indicating the goal from all parts of the maze.

The Turf Maze, Saffron Walden Common

Somerleyton Hall hedge maze

The Jubilee Maze, Symonds Yat

Ceramic tile maze at Warren Street Underground Station, London

Saffron Walden Hedge Maze - *Bridge End Gardens Hedge Maze, Saffron Walden, Essex, England (tel. Tourist Information Centre, 0799 24282); yew hedges, 160 x 80 ft; originally planted 1839, presented to the public by I Fry, MP; restored by John Bosworth and Tony Collins, 1984; re-opened 1991.*

The maze was originally planted in c.1839 in a private garden by the wealthy Gibson family. The layout of Italianate design may have been designed by William Nesfield, and was originally embellished with statues and a viewing platform at the centre. During the mid-19th century the gardens were opened to the public and a 1905 document records that the maze could be entered for the sum of 6d.

By the 1940s the maze was suffering from neglect and in 1983, when proposals for the restoration of the maze and the adjacent gardens were put forward, the hedges were so overgrown that the original plan was unrecognisable. During 1984 the remains of the old maze were uprooted and an exact copy of the original was replanted.

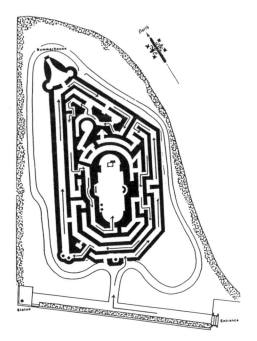

Bridge End Gardens Hedge Maze

Bridge End Gardens and its hedge maze are located between Bridge Street and Castle Street, north-east of the Church; access by footpaths from either and are open free of charge from 9pm to dusk daily.

The hedge maze is ideally located for a combined visit with the Saffron Walden turf maze. Between the two, the Saffron Walden Museum situated in Museum Street is also well worth visiting, and has a good selection of maze books on sale.

Saffron Walden Turf Maze - *The Common, Saffron Walden, Essex, England (O.S. Ref. TL 543385) (tel. Tourist Information Centre, 0799 24282); 450 yards east of the town centre; seventeen-ring Medieval Christian design; brick paths in turf, almost a mile in length; circular with bastions, 132 x 132 ft.*

Europe's largest surviving ancient turf labyrinth is essentially circular, but with four horse-shoe shaped projections giving the maze a total diameter of 132 feet, enclosed by a bank and ditch. The maze paths are brick-paved grooves between turf ridges; the central goal is a 33 foot diameter mound, 18 inches above the level of the paths. An eighteenth century document records *"The Maze at Saffron Walden is the gathering place of the young men of the district who have a system of rules connected with walking the maze, and wagers in gallons of beer are frequently won or lost. For a time it was used by the beaux and belles of the town, a young maiden standing in the centre, known as home, while the boy tried to get to her in record time without stumbling".*

This secular usage, which helped keep turf mazes alive after their religious connections had faded, is rooted in far older pagan practices linked with labyrinths throughout Europe. The first written reference comes from the accounts of the local Guild of Holy Trinity (1699) who paid *"15s.0d...for cutting ye Maze at ye end of ye common".* Further restorations are recorded for 1828, 1841, 1859, 1887 and 1911, when the pathway was lined with bricks to ease future upkeep. The most recent re-cutting was completed in 1979, when some 3,000 of the 6,400 bricks that mark the path were replaced. The maze is in good condition, and open at all times.

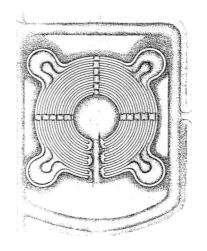

The Turf Maze, Saffron Walden

"Lion Rampant" brick pavement mosaic maze, Worksop

"Unicorn Rampant" brick pavement mosaic maze, Worksop

Saltwell Park Maze - *Saltwell Park, Gateshead, Tyne & Wear (tel. Park Supervisor, 091 478 6405); rectangular, 86 x 46 ft; originally planted in yew hedges by William Wailes c. 1860; later replanted in beech hedges; replanted with yew hedges, 1983.* **Please Note - the maze is still being re-grown and so is not yet open to the public, but it can be viewed from the adjacent raised pathway.**

Scarborough - *Esplanade Maze, The Esplanade, Scarborough, North Yorkshire, England (tel. Scarborough Borough Council, 0723 372351); privet hedges, rectangular, 105 x 72 ft; built 1963.* **Please Note - this maze is not in good condition.**

Scarborough - *Victoria Park Maze, Scarborough, North Yorkshire, England (tel. Scarborough Borough Council, 0723 372351); privet hedges, rectangular, 135 x 100 ft; built 1959.* **Please Note - this maze is not in good condition.**

Scilly Isles - *Troy Town, Island of St Agnes, Scilly Isles, England (O.S. Ref. SV 875078); stone-lined path labyrinth in grass, circular, 24 x 21 ft.*

The only 'ancient' stone labyrinth to be found in Britain is on St. Agnes, the westernmost inhabited island of the Scillies, 28 miles south-west of Land's End. Known as "Troy-Town", it is situated on the west side of the island, south of Troy Town Farm. Tradition records that the Troy Town Maze was laid out in 1729 by Amor Clarke, a local lighthouse keeper. Supposedly he constructed the Troy Town to while away a few hours during a visit to the island; the source of his inspiration is not clear, whether he was simply repeating a local tradition or had seen a similar example elsewhere, maybe in Scandinavia, for there are no known instances of stone labyrinths at this date or earlier, anywhere else in the British Isles.

The Troy Town Maze now has a seven-circuit 'Classical' design 24 x 21 ft in diameter; originally, before (unauthorised) alterations in 1988, it was somewhat smaller. Travel to St. Agnes involves a ferry or flying to St. Marys, and then a connecting ferry. Careful planning and at least an overnight stay is needed to visit the stone labyrinths of the Scillies.

Scilly Isles - *Troy Town, Island of St Martins, Scilly Isles, England (O.S. Ref. SV 923169); various stone-lined path labyrinths in grass, circular and square, various sizes, all late twentieth century.*

There are a number of 'modern' stone labyrinths north of Scilly Point, at the north end of St. Martins, overlooking White Island. Some soon disappear through neglect, but others are maintained by curious visitors and will no doubt become monuments of the future. Currently there are about fifteen, although their sites and designs are constantly changing as tourists plunder the stones from old labyrinths to build new examples, often of curious 'puzzle maze' designs. The earliest maze on St. Martin's was supposedly constructed by bored Second World War aircrew stationed on the island, a story reminiscent of the origin of the St. Agnes Troy-Town!

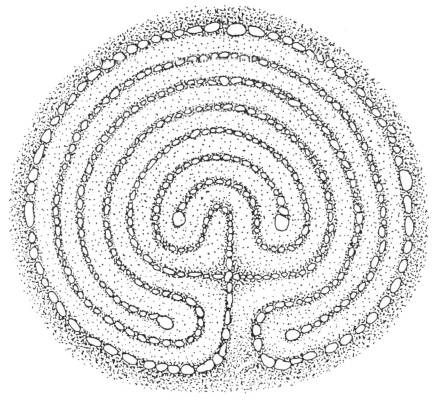

Troy Town, St Agnes, Scilly Isles

The Turf Maze, Wing

The central fountain, Magical Mirror Maze, Wookey Hole Caves

Scone Palace - *"The Murray Maze", Scone Palace, near Perth, Perthshire, Scotland, PH2 6BD (tel. 0738 52300); in shape of five-pointed Murray Star, with wooden bridge; copper and green beech hedges; 217 x 210 ft; maze designed by Adrian Fisher of Minotaur Designs; bridge designed by Vernon Gibberd; to be opened in 1993.*

The Earl of Mansfield's beech hedge maze is in the shape of the family's heraldic five-pointed Murray Star. The maze is planted with interlocking rows of copper and green beech hedges, thus creating a Scottish tartan effect, and has only one straight hedge in the whole

design. The Victorian-style wooden bridge spans four rows of paths, and adds a third dimension to the maze puzzle. Appropriately, it has been laid out on a piece of land known as the Monk's Playground, and is intended to act like a magnet in the landscape, drawing visitors through the formal gardens to the maze.

Shefford - *"Hoo Hill Maze", The White Bungalow, Hitchin Road, Shefford, Bedfordshire (tel. 0462 813475); golden leylandii hedge maze; square, 90 x 90 ft; designed by John Brindle, 1983.*

Somerleyton Maze - *Somerleyton Hall, near Lowestoft, Suffolk, England (tel. 037 984 505); central pagoda on knoll; yew hedge maze, 245 x 160 ft; designed by William Nesfield, 1846.*

The Somerleyton maze was laid out in 1846 by William Nesfield. Its charm arises from the generous scale on which it was laid out, and its delightful pavilion on a large raised mound. The design of the Somerleyton maze was later copied at Worden Park in Lancashire, since both mazes were built for the same family. The yew hedges are the original ones planted in 1846.

Sonning Common - *"The Saxon Maze", The Herb Farm, Sonning Common, near Reading, Berkshire, England (tel. 0734 724220); in the shape of four Saxon sea creatures, with surrounding embankment; beech hedges, square, 165 x 165 ft; designed by Adrian Fisher and Lesley Beck of Minotaur Designs, 1991.*

The Saxon Maze is approached through a narrow defile within an enclosing earth rampart.   The maze has a four-fold rotational symmetry, reflecting the four main categories of herbs - Culinary, Medicinal, Aromatic and Decorative.   Seen from the air, the beech hedges portray four mythical saxon sea-creatures, derived from an 8th century illuminated manuscript. Visitors reach the eye of each creature to discover four of the sacred Saxon herbs, before viewing the entire maze from the central Tump.

Sovereign Centre - *Sovereign Centre, Royal Parade, Eastbourne, East Sussex, BN22 7LQ, England (tel. 0323 412444); 'Minotaur Colour Maze' of interlocking plastic tiles, 32 x 16 ft; designed by Adrian Fisher of Minotaur Designs, 1991.*

Spalding - *Springfield Gardens, Spalding, Lincolnshire (tel. 0775 724843); built to celebrate the Queen's Silver Jubilee; Cupressus leylandii hedges, 75 x 75 ft; designed by Peter Atkinson, 1977.*

Strathpeffer - *The Touchstone Maze, Blackmuir Wood, Strathpeffer, near Dingwall, Ross-shire (tel. 03817 539); north of Inverness; maze of standing stones, each weighing up to 2 tons; circular, 84 x 84 ft; designed by Helen Rowson, 1991.*

Helen Rowson, an active member of Highland Arts and Disability, designed this maze particularly for the disabled to appreciate it.

Swansea - *Rose Hill Quarry Labyrinth, Rose Hill Quarry, Swansea, West Glamorgan, Wales (O.S. Ref. SS 644935); seven-ring Classical labyrinth design; gravel paths in turf, circular, 30 x 30 ft; built by Bob Shaw, 1987.*

This modern turf labyrinth is part of a scheme to develop a long-disused quarry to provide "footpaths, recreational activities and to stimulate interest in the environment". Occupying the site of an old tennis court, the original red gravel from the court now forms the pathway between turf ridges. The footpath that runs past the maze has been diverted to lead the walker in and a large stone at the centre provides a comfortable seat to sit and take in the marvellous views of Swansea Bay.

Symonds Yat West - *Jubilee Maze, Symonds Yat West, near Ross-on-Wye, Hereford & Worcester, England (tel. 0600 890360); Lawson's cypress hedges, octagonal, 135 x 135 ft; created by Lindsay and Edward Heyes, 1981; also Maze Museum, opened 1991.*

Built by brothers Lindsay and Edward Heyes, the Jubilee Maze is a popular attraction in the Wye Valley. The style is that of a Labyrinth of Love, popular between 1560 and 1650, although none now remain. A period atmosphere is created by the brothers dressing in white flannels, blazers and boater hats, and giving a personal greeting to every visitor to the maze. Once inside the maze you are invited to indulge in a gentle game of tag or hide and seek, whilst the brothers may pleasantly surprise you by appearing on stilts, or riding a unicycle. The goal of this fragrant maze is a stone pavilion, floodlit from dusk in August. After solving the maze visitors can enjoy a view from a raised platform, overlooking the maze. There is also an informative Museum of Mazes, and an intriguing Puzzle Shop.

Tatton Park Maze - *Tatton Park, Knutsford, Cheshire, England (tel. 0565 54822); owned by the National Trust; beech hedges, rectangular, 114 x 60 ft; copy of Hampton Court maze, built by 4th Baron Lord Egerton c. 1890.*

Telford - *Wonderland Maze, Telford Town Park, Telford, Salop, England (tel. Children's Wonderland, 0952 591633); central gazebo; beech hedge maze; designed by David Wassell and Nigel Jones of Telford Development Corporation, 1989.*

This maze was based on an Elizabethan maze design for Hatfield House, but with an added Victorian character, by using giant figures from Alice-in-Wonderland.

Temple Newsam Maze - *Temple Newsam House, Leeds, West Yorkshire, England (tel. 0532 647321); brick paths in gravel, rectangular, 114 x 92 ft; 1978.*

Temple Newsam House derives its name from the Knights Templar, who are thought to have had a significant role in the creation of Medieval Christian pavement mazes in the 13th century. This brick and gravel pavement was based on a hedge maze design of 1587 by Jan Vredeman de Vries.

Traquair Maze - *Traquair House, Innerleithen, Peebles-shire, Scotland (tel. 0896 830323); Cupressus leylandii hedges, square, 147 x 147 ft; designed by John Schofield, 1980.*

This hedge maze is laid out on the lawn immediately below the house, and several of the high windows have spectacular downward views.

Warren Street Pavement Maze - *Warren Street Playground, London WC1; uses central 7 rings of 11-ring Medieval Christian design; brick maze, square; designed by John Burrell, 1979.*

Warren Street Underground Station Mazes - *Warren Street, London, WC1; ceramic tile mazes on walls of underground station, rectangular; designed by Crosby Fletcher Forbes.*

Warren Street in central London offers an irresistible visual pun on the word Warren. This striking ceramic black and red tile maze design is used as a wall motif up and down the platforms. The nearby Warren Street children's playground was built later.

Warrington Turf Maze - *Parkfield, Warrington, Cheshire, England (O.S. Ref. SJ 630914); gravel paths in grass, circular, 60 x 60 ft; built 1984.*

Parkfields, a housing estate on the north-east edge of Warrington, is the location for a 'reproduction turf maze'. The maze was constructed in 1984 in a small public park in the middle of the estate (to which there is pedestrian access only) alongside such curious structures as mock stone circles and standing stones, all connected together by gravel path 'ley-lines'! One of these paths leads to a fullsize copy of the hand of the Cerne Abbas Giant hill figure in Dorset, passing through the 'turf maze' en route.

Whitley Bay - *Rocket Maze, Springfield Park, Forest Hall, near Whitley Bay, Tyne and Wear, England; gravel paths in grass, in shape of Stephenson's Rocket steam engine, 100 ft long; built 1984.*

Winchester - *Miz-Maze, St Catherine's Hill, near Winchester, Hampshire, England (O.S. Ref. SU 484278) (tel. Tourist Information Centre, 0962 840500); nine ring labyrinth, based on Medieval Christian design; poorly recut, with path as gulley and turf as barrier; turf maze, square, 90 x 86 ft.*

St. Catherine's Hill, 328 feet above sea level and overlooking the city of Winchester, is encircled by the ditch and ramparts of an Iron Age hill-fort occupied before the Roman invasion. The summit of the hill is crowned by a clump of beech trees which conceal amidst their roots the remains of St. Catherine's Chapel, which stood here from c. 1080 - 1539. A few yards to the ENE of the clump and the buried footings of the chapel lies the Mizmaze, a square turf maze of a curious nine-circuit design which has possibly arisen as the result of various re-cuttings over the years. The pathway is marked by a deep groove worn into the turf, but can become somewhat overgrown in summer.

The age of the Mizmaze is uncertain, for despite its location next to an early Medieval chapel on a hilltop, local tradition records that the

Mizmaze was cut by a schoolboy who, detained at college for the Whitsuntide holidays for some misdemeanour, composed the famous tune of 'Dulce Domum' and carved the labyrinth before drowning himself in the River Itchen which flows past the hill.

Despite its strange unbalanced design, and the rather uncertain history, the Mizmaze remains an essential turf maze to visit, particularly for its atmospheric location and the panoramic views of Winchester. Access to the site is difficult, however, as the busy M3/A33 rushes past at the foot of the hill. Footpaths lead up from the old road across Twyford Down, but the continued extension of the M3 motorway constantly changes the layout of the roads and tracks. Consult a current map or the Winchester Tourist Information Centre for the best route.

The Winchester Miz-maze

Wing Maze - *The Common, Wing, Leicestershire, England (O.S. Ref. SK 895028); eleven-ring Medieval Christian design; turf paths, circular, 50 x 50 ft.*

Known simply as "The Old Maze", the turf maze in the village of Wing, in the old county of Rutland, is one of the best surviving examples. Easily located, it stands beside the road enclosed in a white wooden railing, just to the south of the village sports field. This maze is regularly tended and restored by the villagers and is always a pleasure to visit. There formerly stood in the adjoining field a small bank or mound of unknown age, from which it is claimed spectators would watch the sport of running the maze, but this has now unfortunately been removed. The Old Maze is open at all times, but please park sensibly and respect residents' access.

Wolseley Garden Park - *The Britannia Maze, Wolseley Garden Park, Rugeley, Staffordshire, England (tel. 0889 574766); central stone tower; thuja plicata hedge maze, in shape of Britannia superimposed on the map of Britain, 400 x 200 ft; designed by Adrian Fisher and Lesley Beck of Minotaur Designs, planned to open in 1993.*

The Britannia Maze,
Wolseley Garden Park

For those with any sense of geography, a maze in the shape of a map brings out wonderful sensations of recognition: "I think I'm lost in Cornwall!" "Is this the way to reach Scotland?" This maze will be one of the highlights of Sir Charles Wolseley's new garden park, wittily superimposing the female figure of Britannia onto the outline of Britain. Lady Wolseley, being an American, first arrived by ocean liner at Southampton, which is the entrance to the maze.

The maze design has an unexpected focal point; Britannia has hitched her shield up, so that it is centred on Rugeley. This ensures that the view from the top of the stone tower will be in keeping with Sir Charles' perspective of the world!

Wookey Hole Caves - *"Magical Mirror Maze", Wookey Hole Caves, Somerset, England (tel. 0749 72243); walls of mirrors, with visual deceptions and central fountain, 60 x 30 ft; designed by Adrian Fisher and Lesley Beck of Minotaur Designs, 1991.*

For sheer magic, there is nothing to beat a visit to the Magical Mirror Maze! The deceptions of this beautifully-decorated mirror maze are superb, giving the illusion of spacious avenues of pillars in all directions like a giant colonnade. The goal provides the setting for a magnificent fountain, with over a hundred jets dancing to music; its character continuously changes with marvellous coloured lighting effects. Look out for the apparition of Britain's most famous magician. Children come out of the Magical Mirror Maze simply beaming from ear to ear.

Worldwide, mirror mazes are rare. One of the most famous is the mirror maze in the Glacier Gardens, Lucerne, Switzerland; there are others in Prague, the Musee Grevin in Paris, on Fisherman's Wharf in San Francisco, and at Blackpool Pleasure Beach in Lancashire.

Worden Park Maze - *Worden Park, Leyland, Lancashire, England (tel. Park Manager 0772 421109); hornbeam hedge maze with central mound, same design as Somerleyton Maze (which was designed by William Nesfield, 1846); built by a member of the Farington family, 1886.*

Worksop - *Lion Rampant Maze, Worksop Town Centre, Nottinghamshire, England; brick mosaic pavement maze; rectangular, 45 x 33 ft (13.84 x 9.99 m.); designed by Adrian Fisher, Lesley Beck and Randoll Coate of Minotaur Designs, 1989. The Worksop Town Centre pedestrianisation scheme (including the Lion and Unicorn mazes) won first prize in the British "Street Design 1990" competition.*

Worksop - *Unicorn Rampant Maze, Worksop Town Centre, Nottinghamshire, England; brick mosaic pavement maze; rectangular, 38 x 27 ft (11.75 x 8.23 m.); designed by Adrian Fisher, Lesley Beck and Randoll Coate of Minotaur Designs, 1990.*

The Lion Rampant and Unicorn Rampant brick pavement mazes are keynote features within the Worksop Town Centre pedestrian area. A strong heraldic theme was chosen for the scheme, based on the five Dukeries of Nottinghamshire. Lions appear in the heraldic devices of the Dukes of Norfolk and Kingston, and the Lion and Unicorn are paired as in the Royal Family's Coat of Arms.

Laid in various colours of paving brick, they are exciting designs, and also puzzling mazes to solve. Visitors enter at the foot, and the goal is each creature's head. The maze paths, partly within the body and partly outside, run between the darker lines of the design.

Wyck Rissington - *Maze of the Mysteries of the Gospels, Wyck Rissington Church, Gloucestershire (tel. Great Rissington Rectory, 0451 205600); memorial wall mosaic; 3 x 2 ft; based on design of former hedge maze (created by Canon Harry Cheales) in rectory garden; mosaic designed by Adrian Fisher of Minotaur Designs, and dedicated by the Venerable Eric Evans, 1988.*

In 1950, Canon Harry Cheales had a dream in which he was guided to create a hedge maze in the rectory garden at Wyck Rissington. The maze symbolised the fifteen Mysteries of the Gospels, echoing the wooden carvings still to be seen in the chancel. Each year on the feast of St Lawrence, the church patron's saint, he led a procession through the maze, into the church for evensong, and then outside for a parish supper. When Canon Cheales retired, the maze was removed and the rectory sold. After his death, a wall mosaic of the maze was created in his memory, and installed in the wall of the north aisle of the church. The push-button light will help you see it better.

Yorkshire Dales Steam Railway - *Embsay Maze, Yorkshire Dales Railway Museum Trust, Embsay Station, Skipton, North Yorkshire, England (tel. 0756 795189); small children's maze; maze is only open a few days each year, on days that steam trains run.*

Yorkshire Museum of Farming - *Murtonpark, Murton, York, North Yorkshire, YO1 3UF, England (tel. 0904 489966); small turf maze, based on Dalby design; created by Lis Barratt, 1991.*

British Mazes
open to the public

Strathpeffer ●   ■ Cawdor Castle

Landmark Centre ▲

Hazlehead Park ■
Aberdeen

Scone Palace ■

● Finlaystone

▲ Irvine (2)   Traquair House ■

● Turf Mazes

■ Hedge Mazes

▲ Other Mazes

Burt ▲   Carnfunock ■

Whitley Bay ●
Saltwell Park ■

Scarborough (2) ■

Dalby ●

Leighton Hall ●

Burton Agnes Hall ■

Blackpool Pleasure Beach ■   Hull (2) ▲▲

Worden Park ■

Temple
Newsam
House

▲ Alkborough (3)

Rathmore ▲

● Warrington

▲▲ Worksop (2)

Hollywood Stone ▲

Tatton Park ■

Chatsworth House ■   Doddington Hall ■

Russborough ■

Spalding ■   Somerleyton
Hall ■

Centre for ■
Alternative
Technology
Machynlleth

Wolseley Garden Park ■

Leicester
University

● Wing   ▲ Ely Cathedral

Telford ■

Castle Bromwich ■
Hall Gardens

Hilton ●
Bourn ▲

Hadstock ■

Burford House ▲
Llangoed Hall ■

▲ Ragley Hall

Milton Keynes ●

▲ Kentwell Hall

Saffron Walden (2) ●

Hereford Cathedral ▲

Symonds Yat West ■

Swansea ▲   Cardiff
Castle ■   Caerleon
-on-Usk

▲ Wyck
Rissington   Blenheim Palace ■   Hatfield House ▲   ■ Mistley Place

Chenies Manor ■

Greys Court ●   ■ (2)   ■ Capel Manor

Pennard ▲   Margam ▲
Park   Bristol (2) ▲▲

The Herb Farm ■

▲ Warren Street

Sonning Common ▲

Crystal Palace ■

▲ Batheaston

Hampton Court Palace ■   ■ Leeds

● Bath

Manningford Nurseries ■   ▲ Compton   Castle

Wookey Hole Caves ▲

Longleat House ■   ▲ Itchen Stoke   Hever
Castle ●

Breamore (2) ●●   ● Winchester

Paulton's Park ■●   ▲ Parham Park

Rock Valley, Tintagel (2) ▲▲

▲ Boscastle

Rhinefield House ■   Mayflower Park ■

Merritown   Southampton
House ■

Newquay Zoo ●
Lappa Valley ●
Railway

Dart
Valley
Railway   Bicton Park ■

Blackgang Chine ■

Flambards ▲
Theme Park
● St Agnes   Glendurgan House

● St Martins

United Kingdom - Mazes Listed by County

Aberdeenshire - Hazlehead Park hedge maze (Aberdeen).

County Antrim, N.I. - Carnfunock hedge maze.

Avon - Bath Festival Maze (Beazer Gardens), Batheaston Church pavement maze, Bristol Roof Boss Maze (St Mary Redcliffe Church), Bristol Water Maze.

Ayrshire - Irvine Beach Park maze, Irvine Town Centre stained glass maze.

Bedfordshire - Shefford hedge maze.

Berkshire - Sonning Common hedge maze.

Buckinghamshire - Chenies Manor (turf maze and hedge maze), Milton Keynes (Willen Lake turf maze).

Cambridgeshire - Bourn Church pavement maze, Ely Cathedral pavement maze, Hilton Common turf maze.

Cheshire - Tatton Park hedge maze, Warrington turf maze.

Cornwall - Boscastle slate carving, Flambards Theme Park colour maze, Glendurgan hedge maze, Lappa Valley Railway maze, Newquay Zoo hedge maze, Rocky Valley maze carvings (near Tintagel), Scilly Isles (St Agnes and St Martins).

Clwyd - Bodelwyddan Castle hedge maze.

Derbyshire - Chatsworth hedge maze.

Devon - Bicton Park wooden maze, Dart Valley Railway hedge maze.

Dorset - Merritown House hedge maze (Alice-in-Wonderland maze).

County Durham - Consett giant earth maze.

East Sussex - Drusillas Park colour maze, Sovereign Centre colour maze (Eastbourne).

Essex - Hadstock Churchyard, Mistley Place hedge maze, Saffron Walden hedge maze (Bridge End Gardens), Saffron Walden turf maze.

Gloucestershire - Wyck Rissington mosaic maze.

Gwent - Caerleon-on-Usk roman mosaic labyrinth.

Hampshire - Blackgang Chine hedge maze, Breamore ("Great British Maze" and "Miz-maze" turf mazes), Itchen Stoke pavement maze, Mayflower Park concrete maze, Paultons Park hedge maze, Rhinefield House hedge maze, Winchester turf maze ("Miz-maze").

Hereford and Worcester - Burford House hedge maze, Hereford Cathedral (Mappa Mundi), Symonds Yat West hedge maze.

Hertfordshire - Hatfield House low box maze.

Inverness-shire - Landmark Centre wooden path maze.

Kent - Badsell Park Farm hedge maze, Crystal Palace Park hedge maze, Hever Castle hedge maze, Leeds Castle hedge maze.

Lancashire - Blackpool Pleasure Beach hedge maze, Leighton Hall turf maze, Worden Park hedge maze.

Leicestershire - Leicester University pavement colour maze, Wing turf maze.

Lincolnshire - Doddington Hall turf maze, Spalding hedge maze.

London and Middlesex - Capel Manor hedge maze, Warren Street pavement maze, Warren Street Underground Station.

Nairnshire - Cawdor Castle hedge maze.

North Humberside - Burton Agnes Hall hedge maze, Hull City Hall (roman mosaic labyrinth), Hull brick pavement maze.

North Yorkshire - Dalby turf maze, Scarborough (Esplanade and Victoria Park hedge mazes), Yorkshire Dales Railway maze, Yorkshire Museum of Farming turf maze.

Nottinghamshire - Worksop (Lion Rampant and Unicorn Rampant pavement mazes).

Oxfordshire - Blenheim Palace colour maze, Blenheim Palace hedge maze, Greys Court turf maze (Archbishop's Maze).

Peebles-shire - Traquair House hedge maze.

Perthshire - Scone Palace hedge maze.

Powys - Machynlleth environmental maze.

Ross-shire - Strathpeffer standing stone maze.

Shropshire - Telford Town Park hedge maze.

Somerset - Glastonbury Tor, Wookey Hole Caves mirror maze.

South Humberside - Alkborough Cemetery, Alkborough Church (stained glass window maze and pavement maze), Alkborough turf maze.

Staffordshire - Wolseley Garden Park hedge maze.

Suffolk - Kentwell Hall courtyard maze, Somerleyton Hall hedge maze.

Surrey - Compton (Watts Memorial Chapel), Hampton Court Palace hedge maze.

Tyne & Wear - Saltwell Park hedge maze (Gateshead), Whitley Bay turf maze.

Warwickshire - Ragley Hall.

West Glamorgan - Cardiff Castle pavement maze, Margam Country Park hedge maze, Pennard turf maze, Swansea (Rose Hill Quarry labyrinth).

West Midlands - Castle Bromwich Hall Gardens hedge maze.

West Sussex - Crawley pavement mazes, Parham Park turf maze.

West Yorkshire - Temple Newsam House courtyard maze (Leeds).

Wiltshire - Longleat hedge maze, Manningford maze.

Republic of Ireland - Mazes listed by County

County Donegal - Burt.

Dublin - Hollywood Stone.

County Meath - Rathmore.

County Wicklow - Russborough hedge maze.

Suggested Reading

Titles authored by Adrian Fisher are available by mail order from Minotaur Designs, 42 Brampton Road, St Albans, Hertfordshire, AL1 4PT; titles authored by Jeff Saward are available from Caerdroia Publications, 53 Thundersley Grove, Thundersley, Benfleet, Essex, SS7 3EB. Please write to either address for book lists and mail order prices.

Bord, Janet, "Mazes and Labyrinths of the World" (Latimer, London; 1976). Pictorial guide to mazes and labyrinths, especially in the UK. Now out of print.

Borges, Jorge Luis, "Labyrinths" (Penguin Modern Classics, London; 1962). Stories and essays set in a labyrinthine world.

Coate, R., Fisher, A., and Burgess, G., "A Celebration of Mazes", 4th edition (Minotaur Designs, 42 Brampton Road, St Alban's, Hertfordshire, AL1 4PT; 1986). A general history of the world's mazes, with selected symbolic mazes discussed in detail. Contains 1986 list of mazes throughout the world open to the public. 80 pages, 59 illustrations. Now out of print.

Fisher, Adrian, and Gerster, Georg, "The Art of the Maze" (Weidenfeld and Nicolson, 91 Clapham High Street, London SW4 7TA; 1990). The modern definitive book on mazes worldwide. Introduces mazes and labyrinths as a vibrant and contemporary art form, from ancient mythical origins to modern landscapes. Aerial photographs by Georg Gerster, generally acknowledged to be the world's leading aerial photographer. 170 pages; 100 colour and 30 black and white photographs and 25 line illustrations.

Fisher, Adrian, and Kingham, Diana, "Mazes" (Shire Publications Ltd, Cromwell House, Church Street, Princes Risborough, Buckinghamshire, HP17 9AJ; 1991). An illustrated introduction to mazes, especially in Britain, including their contribution to garden history. 28 pages.

Kern, Hermann, "Labyrinthe" (Prestel-Verlag, Munich; 1982). The most comprehensive reference material for labyrinths of all kinds, though little on modern mazes. German text, 491 pages, 666 illustrations.

Kraft, John, "The Goddess in the Labyrinth" (Abo Akademi, Sweden; 1985) ISBN 951-649-155-3. A well-researched collection of labyrinth myths and legends. Also by John Kraft, over twenty other published works, mainly in Swedish, containing impressive and meticulous research, particularly on Scandinavian labyrinths.

Lonegren, Sig, "Labyrinths: Ancient Myths and Modern Uses" (Gothic Image Publications, 7 High Street, Glastonbury, Somerset, BA6 9DP; 1991); foreword and illustrations by Jeff Saward. A practical workbook, which covers the ancient and mythical past of the labyrinth, and its potential practical uses today. 156 pages, 79 black and white line drawings, 4 photographs.

Matthews, W.H., "Mazes and Labyrinths - their history and development" (1922, reprinted by Dover, New York; 1970). Still a definitive work on Mazes. Well researched, very readable, though inevitably deficient on twentieth century mazes. 254 pages, 151 illustrations.

Pennick, Nigel, "Mazes and Labyrinths" (Robert Hale Ltd, Clerkenwell House, Clerkenwell Green, London, EC1R 0HT; 1990) ISBN 0 7090 4194 2. Substantial history of mazes, from ancient labyrinths to modern symbolic mazes. 208 pages, including 16 pages of black and white photographs.

Saint-Hilaire, Paul de, "Le Mystere des Labyrinthes" (Rossel, Brussels; 1977). A lively if uneven catalogue. In French.

Santarcangeli, Paulo, "Il libro dei labyrinti" (Vallecchi Editore, Firenze; 1967). Thought-provoking study of myths and traditions connected with the labyrinth symbol. 393 pages, 135 illustrations.

Saward, Jeff, (editor), "Caerdroia Magazine" (Caerdroia Publications, 53 Thundersley Grove, Thundersley, Benfleet, Essex, SS7 3EB; over 20 issues since 1980). The journals of the Caerdroia Project are a lively forum for the exchange of ideas, as well as collectively being great source material.

Saward, Jeff, "The Caerdroia Field Guide", 1st Edition (Caerdroia Publications, 53 Thundersley Grove, Thundersley, Benfleet, Essex, SS7 3EB; 1987). Excellent guide to ancient and recent labyrinths throughout the UK.

The Mazes of Minotaur Designs

Minotaur's mazes have been designed by maze designers Adrian Fisher and Lesley Beck; and also Randoll Coate between 1980 and 1986. Opening dates are shown, not construction dates.

Mazes Open to the Public

1. Greys Court - "The Archbishop's Maze", Greys Court, Henley-on-Thames, Oxfordshire; inspired by Archbishop's enthronement sermon, abounds in Christian symbolism; brick paths in grass, circular, 85 x 85 ft; designed by Adrian Fisher and Randoll Coate; dedicated by Dr Robert Runcie, 24 Oct 1981.

2. Lappa Maze - Lappa Valley Railway, St Newlyn East, Cornwall; brick paths in grass, in the shape of Trevithick's steam engine, 161 x 101 ft; designed by Adrian Fisher and Randoll Coate, 1982.

3. Dragon Maze, Newquay Zoo, Newquay, Cornwall; Eleagnus hedges; 210 x 85 ft; designed by Adrian Fisher and Randoll Coate, 1984.

4. Bath Festival Maze, Beazer Gardens, near Pulteney Bridge, Bath, Avon (O.S. Ref. ST 753649); Bath stone paths in grass, elliptical, 97 x 73 ft; circular mosaic centrepiece with six apses depicting aspects of Bath, 15 x 15 ft; maze designed by Adrian Fisher; mosaic design by Randoll Coate; 1984.

5. Tudor Rose Maze, Kentwell Hall, Long Melford, Suffolk; brick pavement, 70 x 70 ft; maze designed by Adrian Fisher; 15 diamond details designed by Randoll Coate; 1985; world's largest brick pavement maze; winner of British Tourist Authority's 1984 'Heritage in the Making' Award.

6. Bicton Maze, Bicton Park, Devon; upright wooden logs, in shape of giant footprint, 160 x 75 ft; designed by Adrian Fisher and Randoll Coate, 1986.

7. Maze of the Mysteries of the Gospels, Wyck Rissington Church, Gloucestershire; wall mosaic; 3 x 2 ft; based on hedge maze design by Canon Harry Cheales, 1950; mosaic design by Adrian Fisher, 1988.

8. Leeds Castle Maze, near Maidstone, Kent; yew hedge maze, with central stone tower, underground grotto and 90 ft exit tunnel; square, 156 x 156 ft; designed by Adrian Fisher, Randoll Coate and Vernon Gibberd, 1988; winner of 1988 Regional Award of the Royal Institute of British Architects.

9. Lion Rampant Maze, Worksop Town Centre, Nottinghamshire; brick pavement mosaic; rectangular, 45 x 33 ft; designed by Adrian Fisher, Lesley Beck and Randoll Coate, 1989; winner of British **Street Design 1990** competition.

10. Unicorn Rampant Maze, Worksop Town Centre, Nottinghamshire; brick pavement mosaic; rectangular, 38 x 27 ft; designed by Adrian Fisher, Lesley Beck and Randoll Coate, 1990; winner of British **Street Design 1990** competition.

11. "Mathematica" Colour Maze, Leicester University, Leicestershire; brick paving 'colour maze', in five colours of brick; square 20 x 20 ft; designed by Adrian Fisher,1991.

12. Marlborough Maze, Blenheim Palace, Woodstock, Oxfordshire; design inspired by stone carvings on Palace by Grinling Gibbons; wooden bridges, and brick and stone pavilions; yew hedges, rectangular, 294 x 185 ft; designed by Adrian Fisher and Randoll Coate, 1991; world's largest symbolic hedge maze.

13. Magical Mirror Maze, Wookey Hole Caves, near Wells, Somerset; walls of mirrors, with visual deceptions and musical dancing fountains, 60 x 30 ft; designed by Adrian Fisher and Lesley Beck, 1991.

14. "Veronica's Maze", Parham Park, West Sussex; brick paths in grass, 96 x 60 ft; designed by Adrian Fisher and Lesley Beck, 1991.

15. Manningford Maze, Manningford Nurseries, Manningford Abbots, near Pewsey, Wiltshire; low box hedges and grass paths, trapezoid shape, 109 x 85 ft; designed by Adrian Fisher and Lesley Beck, 1991.

16. Italianate Maze, Capel Manor, Bullsmoor Lane, Enfield, Middlesex; in the spirit of the 1840s 'Italianate' gardening style; central statuary, stone seating and illuminated fountains; holly hedges, 121 x 88 ft; designed by Adrian Fisher, 1991.

17. Saxon Maze, The Herb Farm, Sonning Common, near Reading, Berkshire; in shape of four 8th century Saxon sea creatures, with surrounding embankment and central mount; beech hedges; square, 165 x 165 ft; designed by Adrian Fisher and Lesley Beck, 1991.

18. **Alice-in-Wonderland Maze**, Merritown House, Hurn, near Christchurch, Dorset; portraying various creatures from the story; beech hedges, octagonal, 240 x 240 ft; designed by Adrian Fisher and Randoll Coate, 1991.

19. **County Mall Colour Maze**, County Mall, Crawley, West Sussex; based on "Hopscotch"; coloured paving tiles, rectangular, 22 x 18 ft; designed by Adrian Fisher, 1992.

20. **County Mall Puzzle Maze**, County Mall, Crawley, West Sussex; coloured paving tiles with central mosaic, rectangular, 32 x 12 ft; maze designed by Adrian Fisher; central mosaic designed by Lesley Beck; 1992.

21. **Murray Maze**, Scone Palace, Perth, Scotland; in the shape of the five-pointed Murray Star, with wooden bridge, copper and green beech hedges, 217 x 210 ft; maze designed by Adrian Fisher; bridge designed by Vernon Gibberd; 1993.

22. **Britannia Maze**, Wolseley Garden Park, Rugeley, Staffordshire; hedge maze portraying Britannia within the shape of Britain, with central stone tower; 400 x 200 ft; designed by Adrian Fisher and Lesley Beck; due open in 1993.

23. **Russborough Maze**, Russborough, Blessington, County Wicklow, Eire; beech hedge maze, with central statue on pillar; square, 142 x 142 ft; designed by Adrian Fisher and Randoll Coate, 1993.

24. **Cheju-Kimnyong Maze**, Cheju Island, South Korea; in

shape of Cheju Island, portraying wild ponies, snakes, volcano and shipwreck, with central tower; Cupressus leylandii hedges; 296 x 140 ft; designed by Adrian Fisher and Randoll Coate, 1993.

Plastic Colour Mazes

1. **Flambards Colour Maze**, Flambards Theme Park, Helston, Cornwall; interlocking plastic tiles, square, 25 x 25 ft; designed by Adrian Fisher, 1991.

2. **Blenheim Colour Maze**, Blenheim Palace, Woodstock, Oxfordshire; interlocking plastic tiles, square, 25 x 25 ft; designed by Adrian Fisher, 1991.

3. **Drusilla's Colour Maze**, Drusilla's Zoo, Alfriston, East Sussex; interlocking plastic tiles, square, 25 x 25 ft; designed by Adrian Fisher, 1991.

4. **Sovereign Centre Colour Maze**, Eastbourne, East Sussex; interlocking plastic tiles, rectangular, 32 x 16 ft; designed by Adrian Fisher, 1991.

Mazes for Special Events

1. **Beatles' Maze**, International Garden Festival, Liverpool (Apr - Oct 1984); brick maze paths in water, 100 x 85 ft; and central 51 ft long 18-ton steel Yellow Submarine; designed by Adrian Fisher, Randoll Coate and Graham Burgess; winner of two gold medals, and one of the top ten Festival awards.

2. **"A*Maze*ment" Colour Maze**, Ashley Gallery, Epsom, Surrey; interlocking plastic tiles, square, 15 x 15 ft; designed by Adrian Fisher, 1986

3. **"Edward's Enigma" Colour Maze**, Tenth International Puzzle Party, London; 1,989

interlocking plastic tiles, rectangular, 17 x 13 ft; designed by Adrian Fisher, 1989.

4. **"Roadshow" Colour Maze**, Royal Society's Pop Maths Roadshow, throughout the UK, 1989-90; interlocking plastic tiles, square, 12 x 12 ft; designed by Adrian Fisher, 1989.

5. **Rolawn Turf Maze**, National Garden Festival, Gateshead, Tyne and Wear, England (May - Oct 1990); turf path maze, 46 x 46 ft; designed by Adrian Fisher and Lesley Beck, 1990.

6. **Great Explorations Colour Maze**, Great Explorations 'Hands-on' Museum, St Petersburg, Florida; interlocking plastic tiles, square, 15 x 15 ft; designed by Adrian Fisher, 1990.

Private Mazes

1. **Apothecaries' Window Maze**, Apothecaries Hall, Blackfriars Lane, City of London; stained glass, 3 x 2 ft; College of Arms, maze design by Adrian Fisher, 1989.

Mazes no longer Existing

1. **"Embryo"**, Bournemouth, Dorset; holly, 105 x 75 ft; private; by Adrian Fisher, 1975.

2. **Roxburghe Maze**, Floors Castle, Scotland; beech hedges; octagonal, 192 x 192 ft; designed by Adrian Fisher and Randoll Coate, 1983.

3. **Magnetic Maze**, Thorpe Park, Chertsey, Surrey; brick paths in grass, 225 x 75 ft; designed by Adrian Fisher, 1984.

4. **Bygrave Maze**, St Alban's, Hertfordshire; Thuja plicata hedges; hexagonal, 80 x 70 ft; designed by Adrian Fisher, 1985.

Profiles

Adrian Fisher and his company **Minotaur Designs** are internationally recognised as the world's foremost maze designers. Minotaur Designs has designed and built over thirty mazes in the grounds of palaces, castles, stately homes, museums, zoos, amusement parks and city centres in England, Wales, Scotland, Ireland, the United States and South Korea, with new mazes planned in Europe, North and South America and the Far East. Each maze is individually conceived to reflect the history and heritage of its location. Minotaur's mazes have won prestigious awards, including two gold medals at the 1984 International Garden Festival at Liverpool, the British Tourist Authority's 1984 "Heritage in the Making" award, a silver medal at the 1990 Gateshead Garden Festival, and helped Worksop win first prize in the UK's "Street Design 1990" competition. Minotaur's mazes have appeared in Scientific American, The Smithsonian, National Geographic World, Der Spiegel, Maison et Jardin and many other international publications.

Adrian Fisher has pioneered brick-path-in-grass mazes, Brick Pavement Mosaic mazes, Minotaur Colour Mazes and Minotaur Mirror Mazes, and is enthralled by the opportunities for puzzles, hidden meanings and challenges that each commission represents. He has authored **"The Art of the Maze"**, **"Mazes"** and **"A Celebration of Mazes"**. As Director of Britain's **"1991 - The Year of the Maze"** Campaign, he has awakened a worldwide interest in mazes.

For more information, please contact Adrian Fisher, Chief Executive, **Minotaur Designs**, 42 Brampton Road, Saint Alban's, Hertfordshire, AL1 4PT, England (tel. 0727 44800; internationally, tel. 44 727 44800).

The Caerdroia Project is a non-profit making organisation founded by **Jeff and Debbie Saward** in March 1980 to provide a focus for the study of mazes and labyrinths. A continually expanding body of information provides a valuable resource for current and future researchers. The journal **Caerdroia** documents the findings, ideas and theories of those associated with the project. It acts as a forum for labyrinth research and re-publication of archive material, as a monitor of current developments in the field, and as a means for all interested in this subject to keep in touch. Caerdroia keeps in contact with researchers and enthusiasts around the world, to build up a clearer picture of the origins and distribution of ancient labyrinth symbols and their descendants.

For further details, and a list of back issues and specialist publications (including the **Caerdroia Field Guide**), please send a SAE to **Caerdroia**, 53 Thundersley Grove, Thundersley, Benfleet, Essex, SS7 3EB, England.